BY MICHAEL LALLY

What Withers (1970)
The Lines Are Drawn (1970)
MCMLXVI Poem (1970)
Stupid Rabbits (1971)
The South Orange Sonnets (1972)
Late Sleepers (1973)
Malenkov Takes Over (1974)
Rocky Dies Yellow (1975, 1977)
Dues (1975)
Sex/The Swing Era (1975)
Mentally, He's a Sick Man (1975)
My Life (1975)
Oomaloom (1975)
Charisma (1976)
Catch My Breath (1978, 1995)
In the Mood (1978)
Just Let Me Do It (1978)
White Life (1980)
Attitude (1982)
Hollywood Magic (1982)
What You Find There (compact disc, 1994)
Cant Be Wrong (1996)
Of (1999)
It's Not Nostalgia: Poetry & Prose (1999)
It Takes One to Know One: Poetry & Prose (2001)

IT TAKES
ONE
TO KNOW
ONE

POETRY
&
PROSE
BY

MICHAEL
LALLY

BLACK SPARROW PRESS
SANTA ROSA · 2001

ACKNOWLEDGMENTS

Some of the work in this collection has appeared in: *All You Can Eat;
Arshile; Beatitude; Blasts!; disturbed guillotine; Forkroads; Gargoyle; The
Hollywood Review; L.A. River Festival Catalogue; Lingo; The Louisiana
Review; Out of This World; The Partisan Review; Poetry Near the Bone; Poetry
Now; Rain City Review; Real Living; Salt Lick; Shell; Shiny; Venice Magazine;
Washington Review of the Arts; Woodwind* and in the plays *Hollywood Magic*
and *The Rhythm of Torn Stars*. Additional poems appear on the High
Performance spoken word CD *The Verdict and the Violence* and on the solo
spoken word CD *What You Find There*. Portions of "The Healing Poem"
appeared in the film *Pump Up the Volume*.

Thanks to Karen Allen, Richard Andersen, Eve Brandstein, Bob Callahan,
The Before Columbus Foundation, Joan Hartgens, David Milch, Hubert
Selby, Jr., and Rain Worthington. A special thanks to John Martin and
Terence Winch and, as always, to Caitlin and Miles, and to my wife Jaina
and our son Flynn.

Black Sparrow Press books are printed on acid-free paper.

LIBRARY OF CONGRESS CATALOGING-IN-PUBLICATION DATA

Lally, Michael, 1942–
   It takes one to know one : poetry & prose / Michael Lally.
    p.   cm.
   ISBN 1-57423-156-1 (paperback)
   ISBN 1-57423-157-X (cloth trade)
   ISBN 1-57423-158-8 (signed cloth)
    I. Title.
   PS3562.A414 I85   2001
   811'.54—dc21   2001035886

TABLE OF CONTENTS

3. *It Takes One to Know One*

IT TAKES
ONE
TO KNOW
ONE

POETRY
&
PROSE

1
Heaven & Hell

It's never right, you know, because it doesn't
have everything in it. So you keep going until
you've put everything you can into it, and
then you're out of it. Then you go on to the
next one.

—*Willem de Kooning*

WHAT?

Who won? I feel like
I'm almost there—what
were we competing for?
"the store" "the farm"
the barn where it all
began—the can of spice—
the nice lips on her face—
the place where we fell
asleep at last in peace &
woke up to the air we
remembered that isn't
there anymore—the emp-
eror has no lungs left—
he's only pretending to
breathe—& as for us—
who won—what?

LOVE

I love your language—
I used to speak it.
I used to see you there.
I was with you, wasn't I?
I mean I was there.
I meant to be you then.
I didn't want to offend.
I always did though, didn't I?
I knew you'd understand.
I think you did.
I never hid a thing from you.
I don't think you did either.
I lied, though I didn't know I did.
I spoke your language.
I learned it from you.
I thought somehow I just knew it.
I know better now.
I love that language still, & how.

OLDTIMERS

for M. G.

I have your picture here, on the back of this book. I remember visiting New York, before I moved back for what I thought was good, and, paying for a book on St. Mark's Place, you leaned in to reveal yourself and I was so impressed with your '60s city ease, earring, and hair and still tall, lank, cowboy's stature.

Then Ted told me about the time someone famous was reading at St. Mark's and a huge madman not only disrupted the proceedings but frightened the reader and everyone else as he threatened to kill the poet, and you brought him down and carried him out.

I always thought of you as a younger, better looking Wyatt Earp. I figured you didn't get me, but I didn't mind. There wasn't anything I wanted from you, I just liked the idea that you were out there somewhere in the heartland after enough of New York City. And then you wrote one of my all-time favorite books—essays about just that, being out there in America's chest.

I was happy for you, to have written it, and for me, to be reading it, and to have it to read whenever. And now here's another, several years later, and it's got this photograph on the back of some oldtimer, and it's got to be you, it's the author and you wrote the book, but I wouldn't have recognized you except for maybe something in the eyes, more from your last book than any fading memory.

Another good book. I'll keep this one, too.

HEAVEN & HELL

1. HELL

Hell is
      no escape.
            And no acceptance.

2. HEAVEN

Ah, heaven.
      Heaven is
            more complicated.

As Merton points out, everyone gets Dante's *Inferno,* but who talks about, or even reads, his *Paradiso?*

A SHORT LOVE STORY

for Hubert Selby, Jr.

I feel so helpless, hopeless, in the face of age when I see the look on the young girl's face as we finally get close enough for her to tell I'm not the hunk she thought I was but instead some gray-faced, middle-aged, could-have-been-the-man-of-her-dreams but too late now she sees my scarred and weary heart through my eyes that once were so proud and honest and now are doing all they can just to see her clearly and oh my God she isn't the young girl I thought she was either, the style and the hair making up for what she lost when they took part of her breast that time but not enough to make up for what "he" didn't leave behind—his heart is somewhere else and she's not sure if it's worth trying anymore, at least not with someone as far beyond the prizes she once knew were hers as sure as I knew she was mine. And as we pass, our hearts ache anyway for what might have been and was, so why not stop, and turn around, and—what? start that shit all over again?

SHOOK UP

What shook me up was
your response, as if my
words were battery.
They're not.

LOVE

In the fading light of a Fall, New York City day, a man, mid-thirties, lying on a mattress on the floor of a small bedroom, raises up on one elbow, obviously weak, sickly. With a great effort he gets out of bed, puts on slacks and shirt slowly, meticulously and, occasionally stopping to rest or hold his stomach, he packs a suitcase and a shoulder bag with clothes and books.

It's night, late, in Rome, where in a hotel room, well furnished in antiques, in a big bed, a woman in her early thirties, redheaded and voluptuous, undresses. She is pensive but unselfconscious in her actions, including dropping her clothes wherever she is when she removes them. She gets into bed and looks through books on a nearby table, picks up a paperback volume on witchcraft, begins reading.

In the New York apartment, the man is making a last minute check of: tickets, passport, gas off, windows locked, etc. The apartment has one other room, a combination kitchen and living room and study, with many books on shelves in precise order. All looks neat, though slightly poor. He puts on an old overcoat, rests one last time next to the telephone, turns on the machine and says into it, "I've gone to Rome for two weeks. You can call me there if you have to at the Victoria Hotel, 1-81-33547, or leave a message if it can wait and I'll be back to answer it before Christmas." The effort has tired him, he breathes heavily as he listens to it play back, then rises, takes a last look around and leaves.

In Rome, she has lost interest in her book or been distracted by the thoughts it has provoked. She lays it down on a table with the pages open and face down, looks through some things and pulls out a script which she opens and starts studying.

In New York, the man sits on the stoop of an old federal-style building. It is dark out, the streetlights are on and people pass by dressed for the cold, little shops still open, butcher, etc. The man takes it all in. A car pulls up and a young Israelite gets out and with a heavy accent asks, "You call Jerusalem Car Service?"

The man nods and the Israelite helps the man put the bag in the back seat. They both get in and the car pulls away just after another car, stopped behind it, begins to beep its horn. As they pull away, the driver turns up the radio, which is playing the oldie Beatles' tune, "Love."

In Rome, the redhead has fallen asleep with the script still in her hand. It slides out of her hand and off the bed onto the floor with a little thud which stirs her. She rolls over, reaches out her hand and turns off the light. Slowly the light from the streetlamps outside penetrates the wooden slats of the window shutters and outlines her voluptuous form under the covers, as the sounds of an airport enter her dreams.

In New York the man is entering a plane, finding his seat, obviously worn out, barely aware of taking off. He has difficulty eating the meal they serve, pushing the food aside, taking a couple of pills, the lights in the plane going out as the movie *Breaker Morant* comes on the screen, the man feeling his head, obviously feverish, the movie and plane ride turning into a dream-like state that confuses images of the scenes in the movie with his own visions of the redhead naked and somehow part of the *Breaker Morant* scenario along with the bright moon in the sky outside the window of the plane until suddenly, the man sits up wide awake and startled as the men in *Morant* are executed. Outside the sky is beginning to turn light.

In Rome the woman is sleeping peacefully as the noise of the awakening Roman street begins to penetrate the bedroom. The telephone rings and with great difficulty she wakes up, answers it, nods, finally says something garbled in Italian that seems to mean "Yes, yes, thank you, okay" and hangs up, looks disoriented and tired, starts to go back to sleep.

The stewardess is taking the man's breakfast. He hasn't touched it. The captain is making announcements about what they are flying over. The man looks down over the mountainous terrain of Southern Europe and sighs.

The woman sits straight up in bed as the phone rings again.

18

She talks in Italian again, something like "Yes, yes, I'll be right there, five minutes, five minutes." Then hangs up and says in English, "Fuck!" and jumps out of bed.

The captain is announcing the impending descent into Rome, the seat belt signs go on, everything is in English and Italian including the captain's remarks. The man looks exhausted, but he's smiling.

The woman is rushing her makeup, putting it on in a slap-dash way. Clothes are scattered around, she is in underpants, no bra, and beautifully styled boots. She finishes her lipstick and pulls on a loose-fitting but sexy, elegant-looking dress. She looks at herself in the mirror and tries pushing her hair into some kind of order then throws on a short fur coat and exits.

The people applaud as the plane touches down. When it stops, everyone gets out and into a vehicle, the inside of which looks like a New York subway car. The man seems to be following the crowd.

The woman is in a car with a driver, in the back seat curled up in her little fur looking out at the Roman suburbs, almost falling asleep.

The man is waiting for his suitcase. Others have picked theirs up and gone. There are a few left. As the remaining bags go around and around the man watches them get fewer and fewer until there is no one else waiting but him and the machine stops. He asks various men in uniforms about his bag, but none speak English. Finally one points to a window behind which another uniformed man misunderstands everything but does use several English expressions in doing so.

As the car pulls into the airport, the woman is asleep in the back seat.

The man is now in an office talking to a man not in uniform who speaks English fairly well and is explaining that the man must fill out this form and when the bag is found it will be delivered to his hotel.

The woman gets out of the car sleepily. The driver is holding the door open for her. She tells him to wait there, in Italian, and enters the airport.

The man is filling out the form.

The woman asks someone, again in Italian, where the flight is arriving, goes to an area where passengers are coming out with their bags, being greeted, etc. She looks around for the man.

The man hands over the form, leaves the office and goes to customs where the uniformed Italian begins pawing through the man's shoulder bag, smiling when he sees the picture of the author on a book is the same as the one in the man's passport. The man doesn't smile but keeps looking at the clock and the doors to the airport lobby that the others have all gone through.

The woman stands alone waiting, looking around anxiously, pacing, stopping another Italian in another uniform asking him about the flight. He looks her over as he answers some nonchalant bit about her having probably missed the man. She spins on her heels and walks away.

The man is finally waved through customs and on through the glass doors leading into the airport lounge. He comes through them to an empty space, looks around, there are people all over and he scans them anxiously, finally spotting a red-haired woman walking toward the exit. He yells her name and can't believe it is really her when she turns and looks around. He lifts one arm and half waves, half salutes her. She spots him and comes running toward him. He walks toward her. When they reach each other, she jumps into his arms and he steadies himself, holds her off the ground, kissing her long and passionately. People smile as they pass them, the men checking out her legs as her dress is hiked up from being lifted off the ground in his arms.

When he puts her down and they take a step back to look at each other, both are ecstatic and maybe a little nervous, and he is obviously weak and tired. She takes his hand. "For a minute I thought you didn't come." "I was trying to find my suitcase; they lost it." "Oh no, what a drag. What're they gonna do?" "They said it'd be on the next flight later today and they'd send it to the hotel with a driver." "Great! Come on, I've got a car waiting." She takes his arm and leads him out to the car. The driver holds the door open for them to get into the back seat.

Driving through the Roman suburbs, they alternate between looking out the window and sneaking glances at each other, sizing each other up, checking each other out, remembering each other. She catches him doing it. "Did you forget what I looked like?" "Not exactly." She laughs a little. "What does that mean?" "Well, you look different." "I got my hair cut, silly." "Oh." "Don't you like it?" "Sure. You look great. It's just... well, different, you know." "Well, you don't look different. You look beautiful. You sounded in your letter like you were dying or something. I didn't

20

know what to expect." "I lost ten pounds in five days. I haven't been out of bed in a week. I'm tired all the time and ... my stomach kills me, I can't even eat."

She looks him over. "Maybe you shouldn't have made the trip." He looks *her* over. "Don't be dumb, nothing could've stopped me." At that she grins, almost "sheepishly," and snuggles close to him. "You'll see, you'll be better in no time, I'll make you better." She looks up at him provocatively, and now *he* grins, almost "sheepishly."

Back at the hotel—an old turn-of-the-century building, kept up very well and stylishly, near the top of the Via Veneto, but a side street, not too much traffic—the driver holds the door open again as they get out. The man almost whispers, "Do we have to tip him or what?" "No, don't worry, he works for the studio, it's like teamsters in the States." " 'The States.' I feel like I'm in a World War Two movie." "Well, you're not the only one in this city who feels that way, it's still a real fact of life here."

They enter the hotel, where the clerk and others greet her. She responds in Italian, "Good morning, good morning. Signor Granito, this is my husband." The man and the desk clerk shake hands. "Hey, how you doin'."

As they go to the elevator, he asks her, "What did you say to him?" "I said you were my husband." "Why'd you say that?" "Because that's the easiest way for you to stay here; how do you think I got the studio to pay for your trip, silly?"

After a pause, as the elevator starts to move, he asks, "How do you say that ... 'husband' in Italian?" She says something that sounds to him like "Amorino."

In the room, the maid has been there so the bed is made and the clothes are piled neatly on dresser and bed and chair, all folded. He almost collapses onto the bed.

"Oh baby, I forgot you're sick. You must be exhausted. Did you sleep on the flight?" "Not really. I sort of had this waking dream or something ... it was all mixed in with the movie they were showing." He looks at her as she moves around the room disturbing the neatness the maids had created. He reaches out and picks up the book on witchcraft, which is still lying open face down, and he picks up an envelope and sticks it in the pages and closes the book and puts it down very properly.

"What was it?" "What?" "The movie." "Oh, some Australian flick about the Boer War where these men are arrested and executed

21

for doing something everyone else was doing and getting away with." "What?" "What what?" "What were they doing?" "I don't know, killing people, I guess. Hey, come'ere."

She goes to him and he pulls her down beside him and starts kissing her and touching her and pulling at her dress trying to get his hands inside it, finally just putting his hand up her dress. She pulls away, breathless and looking bewildered, as though she isn't sure where she is, then says, "Wanna take a nap?" "Yeah, if that means we take off our clothes and get under the covers together." "Okay, go ahead, I'll be right back."

She goes into the bathroom and starts running water. He lies there for a while, listening to the sounds of her brushing her teeth, taking a pee, etc., then he slowly gets up and starts undressing, with an effort. He looks pretty skinny without his clothes. He's wearing no underwear and his body fairly glistens with fever. She returns just as he's finished and he gets embarrassed, trying to hurry to get under the covers.

"What's the matter?" "I'm embarrassed. I look so fucking skinny." "You look beautiful, silly, come on let me see." She pulls back the covers. "Oh honey, you look like a little boy." He grabs the covers back and pulls them over him. "Thanks a lot." "Except where it counts, silly." She grabs his crotch through the covers. "What's wrong with looking like a boy when you're in your thirties? Most men would envy you." He pulls her toward him. "Most men would envy me being here with you, gorgeous." She pulls back and sticks her booted foot in his face. "Here. Help me."

He takes a minute to recompose himself, then pulls her boot off with an effort. "Oooooff." She puts the other up for him to do. "Are you hungry, should we order something from room service?" "I told you I can't eat." "Oh, I'm sorry baby, I forgot. You wait, you'll be eating in no time." "Well, there's this special medication, they don't allow it in ... you know ... 'the States' ... but they have it here. It's called Facigin and the doctor gave me a prescription to get enough to supposedly cure me and take some back in case I have a relapse." "Great. But you won't have any relapse, I'm gonna make you all better."

She crawls under the covers and without taking off her dress goes down on him. He looks confused at first, then alert, then getting into it, until his breathing comes hard, his complexion gets red, he starts mumbling, "Oh baby baby," and "Do it, don't stop baby, do it oh," etc. until he comes. She reemerges from under the covers looking pleased with herself. Then she pulls her dress over her head, drops it on the floor, slips her panties off and gets under the covers snuggling up as close as she can to him. He seems totally exhausted.

"I didn't mean to come so soon. I'm..." "Don't worry honey, I wanted you to come, now go to sleep, you need some rest." "I'm so weak these days." "You poor baby, it must have scared you, losing that weight and being so sick. Did you really think you were dying?" "Well, the last couple of days before I found out it was some weird amoebas, sure, it crossed my mind. I mean I never felt like that before from *anything.*" "Just remember it's a good thing. Your body is getting rid of some poison that's been in there a long time, and it's when you feel the worst that you know you're close to getting out the last of the poison and being healed." "It's little fucking bugs down there eating my food and me too." "Sure. That's what the doctors say, that's the way they see it. But you fell for me, right? It literally knocked you out. You could see that this meant a new life for you and you had to get rid of a lot of old ways of doing things and seeing things and your body did too." "Look, I got these amoebas. The doctor said they're all over New York these days. Asians bring them in and then go to work in restaurants or food stores or... whatever. I'm just lucky to be here where they've been dealing with these things for centuries and have the medication to hopefully get rid of it."

"Does it make you feel like a little boy, being so weak and skinny?" "I thought you said I didn't look skinny." "I mean the way you feel." "Yeah. I feel like I'm about nine years old, you know, big enough to be able to figure things out and know what's going on but not enough to be able to quite take care of myself yet, and when you get sick when you're a nine-year-old boy, you wish you were a baby so you wouldn't have to do anything for yourself." "That's right baby, leave it to momma." She takes his head in her arms.

He pulls away a little. "Hey, I didn't mean that. You asked me how I felt." "Yes. And you told me. Like a nine-year-old boy, who wishes he was a baby. So he can have things done for him by his momma and learn to live all over again." He half struggles to free his head from her mothering cradling and half gives in to it. "It's okay, because I feel the same way baby. I want you to be everything to me, my lover, my brother, my husband, my father, my baby. Now go to sleep beautiful baby, go to sleep." He gives in.

Later in the day he wakes up. She is gone. He gets up, weakly goes to the bathroom, sits down to piss. There is a loud knock on the door of the room, the bathroom door is open. Someone says something in Italian, he doesn't understand. Sounds like a woman, must be a maid. "Not now," he yells. "Come back." She yells something again and he gets up from the toilet, frustrated, flushes it and walks to the door, opens it slightly so only his head shows, but also his bare arm and manner suggest nudity to the old housekeeper. She is pretty, gray-haired and polite. Again says something in Italian. He shakes his head no, says, "No kabeesh, no kabeesh."

The woman comes up to them in the hallway, "No 'kabeesh'? Where'd you learn that?" Then the maid and she have a short conversation in Italian about doing the room later and the maid leaves.

"Where were you?" he asks, as she comes through the door and closes it behind her. "Out." "No shit Sherlock. *Where?*" She laughs. "You don't even hardly know where *you* are, so what difference would it make if you knew where *I* was?" "I just wanna know." He's weakening again, sits down on the bed, then lies back.

"I was getting some cigarettes." "Is that all?" "I had a cup of espresso, okay? Relax." "By yourself?" "Hey! We're not married, and even if we were I'd still do what I felt like it when I felt like it and with whoever I felt like doing it with. Understand?" "Yeah. I understand. Does that go for me too? Huh? With whoever the fuck I feel like?"

"Now wait a minute, nobody's talking about going to bed with anyone else." "No? Then what are we talking about?" "We're talking, you beanbrain, about me having a cigarette and a cup of coffee in the cafe around the corner and talking to an old man about World War Two for ten minutes because I didn't want to disturb the sleep of a sick man, who I happen to love."

"I'm sorry. I just feel a little out of it. You don't know what it's like. " "Yes I do." "No you don't! I can't understand the language and I feel like I have the strength of a fucking flea, you know what that's like?" "You don't think I've been places where I don't speak the language, or ever got sick? Just because I don't believe in giving in to it doesn't mean I never feel it. Jeez."

"Where did you never understand the language? Huh? You told me you speak Italian and French, which means you probably understand Spanish, right? Where the fuck were you where nobody understood English, Italian, French or Spanish?"

"Germany." "When were you in Germany?" "Okay, maybe not Germany. Where did you learn 'no kabeesh' and it's 'no kabisco.' " "I learned it in New Jersey from the Italians that beat my ass every day." "That's not Italian, that's New Jersey. And I was in Brazil."

"What?" "Brazil! That's where they don't speak—" "They speak Portuguese there, that's like Italian and Spanish." "Yeah? For a writer who thinks he's an intellectual you sure are incredibly dumb." "I'm dumb?" "Yes, you're dumb. Sometimes." "*I'm* dumb! Shit."

She lets go of her feistiness, "Aw, come on, honey. You know you're not dumb, and you know I'm not either. We both are the same." "The same? What're you talking about, the same? I grew up in New Jersey." "Yes, but you're not there now. You're in Rome. With me. And we're both in love with each other and it's not New Jersey or Winnetka or yesterday or anybody else. It's us, now, here, and you love me, that's why you're here, right?"

"I gotta get these pills." "Okay, okay, we'll go get them, come on." "I wanna take a shower first. But I'm so fucking weak." "I'll order you a softboiled egg from room service, you can eat a softboiled egg, you told me that's what you've been eating." "Okay." "And some fruit." "Just the egg." "I'll get the fruit for myself." She calls and starts talking in Italian.

Later, he's finishing up his egg and toast. She has taken a bit of one piece of fruit and left the rest. The room is fairly messy. She's finishing putting on an outfit that makes her look sexy and matronly at the same time, sort of horsey sensual. He's dressed in the same clothes, his bag still hasn't arrived. He pushes the plate aside and watches her looking at herself in the mirror. He's obviously pleased, and a little disoriented. She's totally concentrated on herself, but then swings around to him and smiles.

"You ready?" "Yeah, I guess so." "Okay, let's go." They go to the door. Before they open it she pulls a wad of Italian bills out of a pocket and hands it to him. "Here." "What's this?" "So you'll have some money, you know, for the pills, or whatever you want." "Whatever?" "Yes. We have to get you some clothes. You can't walk around in this outfit all day." He looks down at what he's wearing, a little chagrined and defensive about it. But she's already out the door, so he shrugs and follows.

Downstairs she tells the desk clerk they're going out as she hands him the key and instructs him to have her "husband's" bag brought right up to the room when it comes.

On the street the sun is bright, the air crisp and brisk. Groups of older well-dressed Roman men stand around on corners talking, while younger women and men walk the sidewalks, all dressed in the current Roman style. People are checking each other's clothes out constantly, but not directly. He begins to notice this as they walk. She seems oblivious of it, looking into windows or directly at people and smiling. She looks suddenly perfectly "correct" in this place and he appreciates it. She leads the way into a sparkling clean, modern, new pharmacy on the Via Veneto. The druggist speaks relatively good English so the man is able to ask for the medicine himself, showing the prescription from the States, and then paying for it with some difficulty, figuring out which bills are which. By the time they get outside, he is feeling a little more at home. She takes his arm and they stroll down the Via Veneto.

"You want to go to the Spanish Steps and do some shopping. We can get you a suit." "A suit?" "Sure, you need a good suit." "I need a good pair of shoes." "Okay, shoes too." "Well, we shouldn't get too extravagant." "Don't be silly, I'm getting about a thousand more a week than I can spend here, and you can't take it out with you, so we'll buy you some outfits." "I feel like a kid, so weak from being sick, and now taken out to buy clothes for, you know what I mean." "I told you, we're everything to each other, so let me mother you a little today."

"Okay." They hail a cab and go to the Steps.

WRITING

I like this way
of writing. I
always did.

LOVE

She's my friend.
I know what people
say about her.
I read the papers too.
But she never did
those things they say
to me. Or you.
So why do you
have to talk about
her like they do?
She's my friend.

THE MAN WHO WAS TOO SENSITIVE

1

THERE IS NO ONE HERE BUT ME the sign over the man's head says. He finishes washing the dishes, wipes his hands on a towel, and moves to get out of the sunlight streaming in through the window over the sink, almost blinding him. Then he turns to another man and says: "I always feel when the sun comes in like that, which it does almost every day this time of year, it's trying to tell me something."

The other man asks: "What? What's it trying to tell you?" "Hell, I don't know," the man answers. "It's like screaming anyway isn't it? That kind of glare." The man gets out an old poster with Russian words on it and tacks it up with pushpins to block the sun; it works. "When I was a kid," says the other man, "I used to talk to trees all the time." The first man sings: "I talk to the trees, but they don't listen to me."

The other man says, "Yeah. I used to get that a lot. I remember this one guy I knew in high school—we went to different schools together—he got all messed up in an accident once, driving this delivery truck after school. He came by, where we were throwing a football around in the street, and tried to scare us by stepping on the gas and heading right for us. But when he went to slow down, his foot slipped off the brake pedal and the only thing he could do to avoid killing a bunch of us was twist the wheel fast and slam into a tree."

He pauses, as if remembering this vividly. "Before we could even get to him, he'd climbed out through the already broken windshield, his face bleeding like a busted water balloon. When some of us went to visit him in the hospital, they brought a six-pack to cheer him up. His face was all wrapped up from the stitches. Turned out he probably woulda been all right if he hadn't climbed out through the broken glass which he didn't even remember. I actually didn't go to the hospital, I didn't really know him that well. But then I felt guilty, so I went and visited him at his house. His mother said he was up in his room, but when I opened the door the bed was empty. And then he came at me from behind the door, his arms straight out in front of him like Frankenstein. I cracked up, which was his intention of course, 'cause he had these stitches all over his face, like Frankenstein."

The man corrects him, "You mean the monster, Frankenstein was the doctor—" The other man says, "Yeah. Anyway, a couple of years later I'm in this bank in Newark and this little guy is in line in front of me and he turns around and it's him. His face still scarred but pretty much healed, and he says to me—'I hear you're talking to the fucking trees these days.'"

The other man stops speaking, as if finished. The first man looks at him, waiting, finally says, "So? What did you say?" "I said 'I always talked to the trees, man.'" Again the first man prods him: "What did he say to that?" The other man looks at the first man, as though it's obvious, and says, "He laughed, and turned back around in the line and never said another word to me until he left. Then, as he passed me on his way out, he sang that riff you just sang."

They're both silent for a moment, as if thinking about all this. Then the first man says, "I always thought of you as sort of a Fonzie type in high school, only cooler, like you are now." The other man frowns and says, "When I was being called—" he waves two fingers of each hand in the air to indicate quotes—" 'a revolutionary' in college, somebody wrote on the wall of the men's room in the bar where all the hip students hung out, that I was—" he waves his fingers in the air again—" 'cool.'" I thought it was a put-down." The first man's incredulous: "Putdown? How?" But the other man still frowns, "I don't know, I just thought they were being ironic or something." The first man says, "That's just because you were in college."

The other man seems to be thinking about that for a minute. But then it's obvious he isn't when he says, "Maybe I should call her." The first man shifts gears with him, "Why? She was making you unhappy—And you know you'll have another one soon, just as good-looking, or better." The other man gets defensive. "I'm glad you're so sure." The first man retorts, "You know you always have a girlfriend and they're always interesting and good-looking. And when it's over, you always do this routine, like you've got this burden of sensitivity to bear, when everybody knows the next time they see you, you'll have another woman, while the rest of us will be wondering if we'll ever get laid again."

The other man seems hurt. "This is for real, man, you saw her, she's incredible." But the first man's not buying it. "She's just another woman, a little better looking than most, but when I saw her I didn't like the way she was treating you." "What do you mean?" asks the other man. "She wasn't looking at you. I watched you together, and all she cared about was who was looking at her or maybe at both of you, but she wasn't watching you." The other man's defensive again, "So? That's what people do at parties." But the first man's not letting up: "No. If a woman is in love with you, she's supposed to look at you to see if you're having a good time or not, to see if you're okay. The way you were looking at her."

The other man almost seems contrite as he tries to explain, "I just got insecure. Man, she called me every night like clock-work, and all she could talk about was how much she was thinking of me, I mean, here she was in New York having dinner with people like Richard Gere or some big producer—" The first man interrupts him, "Richard Gere?"

The other man continues, "Yeah—about this movie or some-thing. Anyway, she's calling me when she gets back to the hotel and it's still early and she's wishing I was there and seeing me everywhere, and then one night I go out with Ed and these two bimbos he's got and all I'm thinking about is how I wish I was home to get her call, you know, but I'm not, and when I get back she already called and when I call her they say she said she doesn't want to be disturbed and I say you mean by everyone but me and they say, 'No, she didn't make any exceptions.' So I stay up so I can call her before she goes to the set and she says, 'What are you doing up so early?' And I make up some romantic riff like, 'The moon is full and it's whispering about you,' and she senses where I'm coming from, the insecurity, and says, 'Look, I gotta go to work.'" So I'm even more insecure. So I arrange for this poet I know to bring her three dozen flowers all in shades of blue and then she doesn't call that night and when I call her she says, 'Look,

31

you're pushing it.' I tell her 'Hey, I'm just scared, we got this thing going and I'm afraid I'll blow it,' and man it's already blown."

"What's blown?" the first man asks, rhetorically, then goes on to answer his own question: "The woman is an ambitious, ruthless, relentless user, and there was nothing she could use you for except to be seen with somebody hip and cool who's nobody's fool and who everybody envies." The other man looks genuinely surprised by this: "Envies? Why?" The first man seems frustrated with the other man's lack of self awareness: "Because you end up with women like her and you don't get burnt." Now the other man's reaction is almost angry, "What do you mean? I'm sitting here with third degree scars on my heart." But the first man won't give in, "You're sitting there, the first guy she ever went out with who isn't gonna nurse a broken ego for two years or the rest of your life." The other man's almost pouting now, as he says, "How do you know?" But the first man just says, matter-of-factly, "You don't have that kind of ego."

The other man thinks about this for a minute, then finally responds: "I don't know. I felt like strangling her." The first man smiles, "That's a good sign." The other man doesn't seem to notice as he continues, "There were things about her—I loved her accent—and her mouth—but her ass somehow—I don't know—like a big baby's." The first man starts to ask: "You felt like strangling her because her ass was like a—" But the other man interrupts the question: "No, not that, that was just something that I worried about, you know, because I always had this thing about asses, you know. That's why I was so obsessed with black women when I was younger, one reason anyway. I mean I always notice eyes first—and there's so much more important than whether a woman has a nice ass with those perfect curves like crescent moons—"

He stops himself. "I hate to sound like the typical man, you know—leg man, ass man—" The first man adds, "—mind man, background man, job man—" But the other man ignores the man's interruption as he continues, "I felt like strangling her," then he suddenly screams: "BECAUSE ALL SHE CARED ABOUT WAS HER AND HER FUCKING FEELINGS!" He stops, calms himself down. "When she wanted to eat, she ate. When she wanted to exercise, she exercised. When she wanted to watch TV or read a book or visit her girl friends or go to the beach or smoke or dance or shop—SHE DID IT!" He's screaming again, calms himself down again. "And when she was done doing whatever it was she felt like doing, she wanted my undivided attention—no matter what *I* wanted. Or she wanted me gone. And she thought if she asked me how I was, that was being sensitive—or listened to me rap about the shadow government or the drug trade or TV evangelists—or whatever—that was the extent of her duty to me. Mine never ended, until she got hungry or tired or bored or whatever. Man, what the fuck do women want?"

"Everything," the first man says. The other man hears him this time and adds, "Except men who are too sensitive." The first man is smiling again as he says, "Well, you don't have to worry about that."

2

DON'T THINK ABOUT IT is printed like a sign on the wall of a small apartment—very much in the old "garret" style of pre-1970s Greenwich Village, only it's uptown. A black woman, same age as the men above, very regal and striking in her manner and appearance, is talking to the other man. "But you and me will always attract people younger than us—because we look so young ourselves. Like I met this guy in Central Park, on my walk—beautiful man, but much younger. We had this wonderful time together, rented some rollerskates, lots of laughs, had a late lunch—very charming man—then he walked me back here, and just as I was getting ready to invite him in, I remembered these pictures I had on the table—of my daughter's wedding. He's too observant not to notice, too polite to ask, but too intelligent not to figure out how much older than him I am."

The other man asks, "So, what did you do?" "I let him kiss me, and then I let him get away." She smiles, as she continues. "That's why I say, get it while you can and enjoy it for as long as it lasts." The other man seems confused by this: "I thought you said that because—" She interrupts his question, "Well, yeah, because I broke up with my boyfriend too soon, just because I knew the age thing was coming up." The other man says, "But you always went with guys younger than you."

"Except for you," she responds. "But that was different," he says, "I was the first. Wasn't I?" She sighs. "You never change, you know that?" He huffs, "No—I don't know that." "Well, don't act like I insulted you, that's a compliment," she sounds exasperated. But he still sounds insulted as he says, "What? That everything I've been through, all the lives I've lived, don't count for anything?" "They count," she answers, "they just don't show. You don't know what a woman would give to be able to live the way you have and not have any of that show."

He asks, sincerely, "What about *us*?" "What *about* us?" she says. "I still think you're beautiful," he tells her, looking directly into her deep brown eyes. There's an awkward pause, but he ignores it. "I miss you." She smiles, says teasingly, "What about Miss—" But before she can even finish, he's down again, "She left me." It doesn't throw her though, "You always say they left you, which is very hard to believe." "Well, you left me—it started a pattern—because you were the first."

She isn't buying into his self pity, "What about Dee?" "That was just teenage stuff," he says. "You were the first real lover I ever had. I mean, I really fell in love with you." She still isn't buying. "From what I've heard over the years, you fall in love more than anyone in the world." But he won't let it go. "Looking for what we had." "Have you found it yet?" she challenges him. "No. Never." "Maybe we didn't really have it then, except in your head." "What about *your* head?" he says, again, sincerely.

"Life has been too busy and too hard to think about the shoulda beens and coulda beens and woulda beens—" She pauses long enough to give him pause, then: "That doesn't mean you weren't my first lover, and that I don't think about you, and how sweet you were—and crazy." They both know she's soothing his ego now, but he can't help enjoying it. "Yeah—we were both pretty crazy back then weren't we?" he says, smiling. "I suppose I was then, but seems like you still are. Like I said, you never change." Oops, she stepped on his ego again, unintentionally, of course.

He reacts: "I've lived in thirty-two places since then, been married and divorced twice—changed careers seven times—lived with three women out of marriage—had too many other lovers to count—of every size shape color religion background—and even—once—gender. I've been up and I've been down—I've been hot and not—in and out—beautiful and ugly—out of shape and almost perfect—through every kind of change anybody has ever written about—and you're telling me I never change?"

She's still calm and regal in her response: "What can I say? You're always you—to me. When you called and said you were in town—it's like I just saw you yesterday. And you walk in and tell me about your latest love, and how your heart is broken, and how your latest career didn't turn out the way you planned—and all the rest—and it's just like it really is yesterday—all the yesterdays we've been talking on and off about, all our lives, to each other. Although we're grown, we still don't own our homes—and you're still roaming the world looking for something you think we had but when you tried to get it back with me—you found out it wasn't there."

"No no, it wasn't that. Hell you even smell the same. I told you that. Every nook and cranny of your body was familiar. And every move you made reminded me of what I've been trying to recreate all these years with other women—but, you started laughing—" She interrupts him, "So did you, it was funny." He nods, "It felt funny—the same and yet not the same—like some old folks had ingested us."

Now *her* ego's been stepped on. "What?" He tries to explain, "Like—I mean—it was you—and me still—all the familiar moves and odors and textures and all that—but the shapes—and the way they feel—there's a softness, a generosity of flesh we didn't have back then." She's got her own spin: "We were a couple of skinny kids fresh out of high school, wired on life and love and the city back then." "And each other," he adds, "why did you leave me?"

"I didn't leave you. You spent most of your time dealing with your family—that sister of yours, and your father—and running back and forth with your friends—and trying to be a jazz musician and a bad street legend and what not." She says this almost dismissively, but that's not what he hears as he answers her with: "See? I have changed. I haven't played piano in years, and I certainly don't run the streets trying to—"

She interrupts him, still not letting him get away with it: "But you weren't really running the streets then, were you? You were running them in your fantasies." "What? I slept in the park, didn't I? Wasn't I running with—" She interrupts again, "But it was romantic then, because we chose to live that way. And what I mean when I say you haven't changed is that you still make choices like that. You still base your choices on some romantic notion of what life might be—not on what it is."

"What is it then?" he asks. "I don't know," she says, about to dismiss the whole subject. But then she gives in and answers with: "Impossible to survive—I guess. No. That's too glib. I just know it's not as perfect or as easy as all that romantic kind of thinking tries to make it." He's defensive again, "Well, you know, I've been *living* too—I haven't just dreamt the last two decades." She says, "Yes, I know." Then, unable to keep it up, she changes the subject: "So, you hungry?"

3

DANTE'S SIDEWALK CAFE, one of the few vestiges left in the Village of the original Little Italy atmosphere. The black woman and the white man sit outside, at a tiny table barely big enough to hold two cappuccinos. The few other sidewalk tables are full of the usual array of New Yorkers, and the sidewalk's busy too. But still there is an air of "old world" here, of a more peaceable neighborhood than the city usually offers. Through the window can be seen a painting of Dante clutching his heart as he spies Beatrice crossing one of the many Florentine bridges.

The black woman looks around her, as though she's visiting a foreign land. "I forgot how peaceful it is down here," she comments. The man says, "Romantic too, you and me, here, after all these years." Again, she isn't buying into his fantasies, "Well, I don't know how romantic it is. As I remember it we had a hard time getting served here back then." Once again, he's on the defensive: "Yeah, well, I didn't mean this place so much as the neighborhood."

But she's creating her own romance, "Washington Square Park—now that was romantic, walking through there again—I remember sleeping in that fountain." "Yeah, back then we could," he says, growing angry, "now all those goddamn dealers make me so mad I want to just blow them away." "That's nothing. Those boys are almost entertaining compared to what we have uptown now. You know how rare it is for me to go out in my own neighborhood at night anymore?"

The man reaches for her hands, holding them in his. "Your hands are still beautiful." She takes them back. "Well, that's nice you think so." "Hey, don't dismiss it—I'm serious. They're even more beautiful now than they were back then. I love it when women's hands get all strong looking as they get older, but are still so obviously a woman's hands. I could look at your hands for hours."

She ignores the compliment as a very black man, a street person who looks like he's obviously homeless, half staggers up the street and when he spots the white man and black woman at a table next to the little railing separating them from the sidewalk traffic, he leans over it and says to them: "How you all doin'?" She looks at the white man: "You know him?" He answers, "No." The street guy ignores their exchange, maybe he hasn't even heard it, as he asks, "Got a cigarette?"

The white man hands the street guy a cigarette, to the black woman's obvious disapproval. The street guy says, "Got a match?" And as he lights the cigarette, the black woman gives him a cold stare and says, "You could at least say thank you." The street guy gives her an equally cold stare back, as he says, "Thank you for what?" He suddenly seems a lot more sober than when he was staggering up the sidewalk.

The white man, trying to defuse the situation, says, "It's okay." The black woman ignores him, her attention still coldly on the street guy, as she tells him, "Go on, you got your cigarette." But he's not going anywhere. He smirks at her, as he blows smoke out of his mouth and says, "Oh, you all siddiddy now bitch, sittin' here with your—" The white man interrupts him, "All right, man, that's enough." Now the black street guy focuses his attention on the white man. "Oh, you don't remember me now, right? You want me to get lost, but you the fool is lost around here, I'M HUNGRY MAN!"

The black woman is disgusted now, turns her chair away. The white man is frustrated, isn't sure what he should do, isn't sure if he in fact actually knows this guy from the old days when they all ran the streets in his mind. Fortunately, he's saved by a short stocky gray-haired Italian man who comes out of the cafe and goes right to the street guy and puts a strong hand on his arm as he looks at the mixed couple and asks, "You know this guy?" They shake their heads.

The Italian man says to the street guy, "Come on let's go, move along," and starts to pull the street guy away from the cafe. With an almost charming smile, the street guy says to the couple, "Come on you all, tell him—we're old friends." He points at the white man, "I know this guy—he's my patty cat, right man? Where you been man—Come on, TELL HIM!" The Italian man ignores all this, starts pushing the man. "I said move it, buddy, now."

He almost knocks the street guy down—even though the

homeless guy is bigger—as he pushes him forcefully. The street guy suddenly starts to cry, big sobs, sounding like a little kid in tears. "Why you wanna do me like this, huh? I ain't hurt nobody— I got no place." He looks pleadingly at the black woman, "You remember me sister, don't you? I'm sorry—I'm sorry—I'm sorry." He finally wanders away, the Italian man making sure he doesn't come back. When the street guy is finally out of sight, the Italian man goes back into the cafe shaking his head as though amused by this city.

After what seems like a long moment of silence, the white man says to the black woman, "You didn't know him, did you?" "Him? No. Did you?" "No. He sorta reminded me of Smokey though." She frowns, says, "Smokey died." "Oh," the white man looks genuinely upset, "that's too bad." But the black woman says, "Why?" Now the white man is really upset. "What do you mean why? Because—it's sad when people you know die." She gives him a look, almost the same smirk the street guy gave her, but it works on the white man, he calms down. Then asks, "What'd he die of?"

"He O.D.'d," she says, "he was a mess. Last time I saw him was at the clinic. I took my daughter in, this was a few years ago when she was still a kid—and this nasty character starts hitting on her—and it's him. I try to cool him down—but he gets all nasty with *me*. That's when I recognized him and said his name—and you know what? He acted like nothing had happened."

THE POINT

Well, what's the
point reminiscing
about the air that
I once drew, so
pure, so free, so rare
these days of where
we all live now
so what's the
point of pointing
out how everything
has gone to hell
if this is where
we live now then
let's live, now.

UNRELATED TO OUR LOVE

I'm tired. And I'm
happy, in an uncertain
kind of way. This
day is almost done,
and so much has oc-
curred I never expected.
What did I expect? To
be alone and quietly
contented with some words
in a book. To stop
worrying about so much.
To know for certain
you are my love and
that that matters more
than it seems to. But
instead, things happen
unrelated to our love or
any other in my life.
Just things, in the world,
and me in there too.
And now these calls for
you and some more things
to do unrelated to our
love. And somehow I'm
relieved, as if I had just
read another good book.

A Fanatic Heart

She thought I said "frantic"—no—"fanatic"—the word "fan" comes from—which is something like passion—or obsession, like the kind portrayed in *Damage* which she loved because it was relentless—there was no way out of where obsession takes us—to the edge of never caring about consequences until it is too late & we can contemplate our next great epic—ALL THE THINGS I'VE TRIED & FAILED AT—except passion—obsession—the kind of "frantic love" that had me scurrying around your life, like laboratory mice in some experiment that thinks it knows more than the mice do—as if they had no feelings worth considering—as if I did too—that's what it means when I turn my heart over to you as though I could—as though it didn't matter—as though I weren't in love with love itself because it shatters all concerns with petty labors of love, the kind we rarely speak of when we speak of love— like making the beds we lie in—lifting each other up to the dreams we fly away in when the day is done & the need to be one with another is overwhelming & all that prevents it is pride—that image inside of what we deserve, only the best—except when we're sure we deserve only what's less than our own lowly selves we despise for being alone again—when all we wanted to do was love you like you'd never been loved before—open the door to your fanatic heart & see it standing there in the air of caring only for us, the way we never could or dared to do—a fanatic heart is all I want from you—& me too.

But maybe that's not what it means—maybe it means the hearts of those who rape and torture little girls and helpless women in Bosnia today—maybe it means that kind of fanatic who

41

can justify an act so cruel we call it "heartless" as though a heart would be incapable of such a thing—but these boys & men have hearts just like the rest of us, and maybe in the past, more peaceful times, looked at those girls like we look at the ones we fantasize about, or send our Valentine's Day cards to, or write our crazed obsessive poetry about when we feel something now called "co-dependent," as if a word like that could ever describe the confusion of fear and passion we feel inside when we fall into love like it is the void there is no returning from—but there is, and we do, and you're thinking wait a minute he can't compare my passion for someone I love or even am only obsessed with to the rapists and torturers of little girls and helpless women, the murderers and thieves destroying Bosnia as we speak—they must have different hearts that we don't want any part of—their hearts are evil, not like ours, or like the men and women whose neglect has created a generation of rapists and torturers, murderers and thieves over here, not like those who work for companies that go right on killing the earth and what has lived on it for millenniums, like the air and the trees and the creatures no one sees but some day may have to rely on for survival—not like those of us who write or direct or shoot or score or make look real the violent fantasies of those of us who are so tough we take our mayhem, rape, and killing, sitting down in some dark communal acceptance of the evil place we pay to be a part of, or on our own favorite chairs or couches falling asleep to the rhythm of destruction and compulsion and repression of the life force that created all we think we want to live for when we think we do—not me—not you—our fanatic hearts pulse only for the love we feel—not the deal that might make us rich in which we get to sell our principles for whatever is the going rate and hate ourselves at some later date when we see what we have contributed to, if we ever do.

I'm not throwing stones here—my house is made of glass too—I want to go and do to those supposed Serbs what they have done to the girls and women who tell these horror tales—but first I've got to take part in a horror story here in some video or TV show or movie or novel or play or poem from a heart as full of failure and the fear of it as mine—it is time as it always has been, to recognize our hearts in all we desire and despise, time to ignite the fires of a force that will not stop loving even what it hates and no matter who hates us—wait a minute, you're thinking, didn't that idea cross our paths so many times before and where did it get us then?—the end of at least officially and legally defined segregation of the races here, oh I don't care if it did fail, what's the alternative? to pick up a gun and blow away the bad guys? I grew up in a family full of cops, I know what bad guys do and look like—they look like me and you and do what we do only sometimes with a twist that makes it worse or more obvious—so isn't it worth trying anyway—just for this one lousy death-filled life-defying-yet-no-denying-we-are-still-alive-and-here-together-our-hearts-filled-with-fear-or-not day?

What do you say we start a fanatic lonely hearts club for the human race to finally face its true significance in all this—that the heart we share in common with the rest of the universe is only energy, whether it's the kind that ignites the frenzy some mistake for passion—or the kind that weighs us down so much we want to sleep forever or at least ignore the acts that are so fucking cruel—literally—fucking—cruel—& I know rape is no act of sex but one of power—obviously—they didn't feel free to do this for the years of living peacefully together—but still, the women who survive wonder if they will ever be able to have sex again with any men—so, it has to have something to do with sex too—oh God what heart is so fanatic to believe that acts like these can be forgiven or somehow justified—sometimes the rapists are boys and men the girls have seen before, or even know—more likely not—just "Serbs" from somewhere else—the local ones ignoring what goes on or taking part or trying to help the girls escape—another kind of heart that maybe is fanatic too—what's new in all this? certainly not the evil these acts make live—it's been alive before in hearts across the globe—the gun-toting kids in limousines, I mean Somalia—yeah—it's tough all over—but not for us—not yet in that way—just tough getting through the day I have to stop writing about now.

Who Are We Now

We are too tired to figure this one out—
We want someone else to do it for us—
We want to be told what it's all about
and not have to pay any attention—
We want to have sex with everyone we meet
almost, but not risk death by having sex
with anyone—We want a relationship
that will last forever if only the one
we're in will come to an end so we can
find the right one—again—We want
to be poets and actors and songwriters
and directors and politicians and saviors
and gods—but while we're waiting for
all that to happen let's just see how
much fun we can make of all those other
poets and actors and songwriters and
directors and politicians and saviors
and gods—We want it all but it's
just too much—We want each other but
we feel like we're being suffocated so
we just want to be alone so we can spend
all our time on the computer or phone
with someone else who is also alone—
We want our own homes if somebody else
will clean them and care for them and
maybe even pay the bills—We can take
care of ourselves as long as we really don't

have to, because then we're so tired of
doing just that we have to get a cat or
a dog or several of each and birds and
pigs and take up smoking the cigs again
until we're so crowded with plants and
electronic devices we have to find some
one to share all this bliss but none of
them seem to know how to kiss anymore
and we're not so enlightened that we
want to be bored with the lovers we're
prepared to change a few things for
as long as they're willing to change
everything for us—not because we
want to control them, we just want
to make sure they really love us,
because now we're not so sure we
really love them but it's too much
trouble and time and energy and risk
to start this shit all over again with
someone new—so we will be whoever
they want us to for a while until we
can get them to be who we wish we
really were back when we knew who
we wanted to be by now—ourselves,
only better.

SEX AND SURRENDER

You make me sick
as in feverish and
out of sorts and on the brink
of nauseous surrender to
this burning desire.
You've been there
in that childhood sickbed when
your head was leaving the pillows and
sheets soaked through from the
fever sweats and all you wanted to
do was surrender to the fever and
the sick feeling, let your body do
whatever it felt it needed to
move through the crazy passion
of disease to something transcendent
in its pure compulsion to release
and purge and indulge in it all
without guilt and responsibility
or image and self-discipline
or commitment and surrender
to anything other than
what has created this shame.
Does it make you nervous,
the language that I choose
to use, remind us both of darker
desires, like the ones that kept
us tied to beds and heads and

gutters and alleys and oh yeah
death and madness unsublime?
My view of what I want from you
has got to do with the sublime.
The sublime reality of no more
shame for these burning desires.

LOVE

Reading Jimmy S., my name surprises me again. I think of Tim. The men I loved I never made love to: Terence, Tim, Jimmy, Ted, Charlie, Clifford, Mel & all the rest. Oh, some, a very few I did, when I was in my politically correct feminist phase in '72-3-4, like Joe, and John & David, and Matthew, Duncan, others I don't recall. But not the one who got me on that roll.

I didn't see him for so many years. And then one night he appears in the house I rented and had lived in for so long and all I could think of was his blood flowing or mine. I wanted him dead and the house, now contaminated, burned to the ground with everything in it. And then I gave up and almost cried, thinking, All right I'll kill myself.

As always, Cubby set me straight. Told me to look inside, find what I hid there long ago, ashamed to know it until now. Just this: I felt like I had been abused, even though I'd given my consent, gave in to what I thought later had been inevitable. But still I felt like I'd been raped, inside, but thought that ridiculous for a thirty-year-old married man to feel.

In poet's stoned delight in life, I celebrated my new commitment to a victim's life, until the lie grew too heavy for my soul. But still, I fooled around in almost sexless ways with Joe, because he was so quiet and unknown. I thought it was a way to know. But even that grew old.

I married again, then moved to where I'm writing this from. My place in the sun. My books got me so many kind and flattering letters and spoken words until my life began to contradict them. In someone's eyes, then mine. I always thought I had too much to explain, again and again, until I finally stopped trying.

Then, that night, he's standing in my living room, then sitting, explaining how he had no idea I was living there. I didn't believe him. Especially later when I moved, and he showed up on my street saying he just moved there himself. And then Clinton got elected and confused himself and moved to make things better until they got worse.

And plans were made for marches and reunions and I was called and asked if I'd be coming back as one who had been there when it all started. I was polite but nervous that they still knew where I was. Like that day at Midnight Special when we cruised the newer books and I got proprietary again about the past when books about my times I thought I should be in I wasn't.

Until I picked up one to make you laugh and said I'm probably in this one and I was, my birthday noted in *The Book of Gay Days*. And it did make you laugh, and wonder what those who knew you might say if they found out you weren't just dating an older man but one who once ran with the men who prefer men, because he thought they preferred him and he thought he needed that.

I guess I did. And now it's long past. And many of them are dead. But you are young and female. And I am alive and as in love with that and all I ever longed for in women as ever. And I forgive the world and me for not being perfect. Do you understand?

There is no grand plan in my head anymore. All the doors are open and there's nothing left to hide. I fell into a trance of political idealism, as if the urges I repressed in marriage, to move on to be with every woman I ever was attracted to were somehow—but what's it like to say it now?

Yes, I loved men I never was that way with, as I love so much else that makes life seem worthwhile: my kids, grown now, my books, the music that reminds me of my potential to be more, the moment when the lights go down in the theater, movie or play, and yes it was sometimes fun to be with someone who shared my anatomy.

But the images of ideal loves, the fantasies and realizations of sexual fulfillment are and were for me with women. And yet I read journals, today, I wrote during that crazy communal sex-wish time and the lies are unique and believable, even though I know what I was struggling with.

What I was struggling with was the desire to experience it all, embrace the possibilities of our truly being one. Now I know better, and yet it's still true. The tree, the breeze, the cloud, the young woman skating by, the gentle child's eyes, the inside of the TV or sound of movie music in our ears.

The energy is real. It's in us all. There is no death, no gender, form, shape, even decision that matters after all. But for now it is now, not after, and we are us, not all, except in flashes of acceptance when we're free. I'm just me. But much less driven by the need to prove it to you.

2
Loose Canon

We are trained to discover our identities as
products of all we prefer: we are the sum of
our preferences.

—*Robert Kelly,* In Time

EVERYTHING

Slower. No, more space between the speed. Time to think about it, regret, fantasize, contemplate suicide, or deaths, or mega-deaths. The loss of parents, lovers, spouse, kids, self. Attending funerals, seemingly stoical, being pitied, avoided, responded to, respected, better than the living.

He is 22 years old in 1964. This means 13 in '55 and 30 in '72. A hell of a time to be knocking about, getting to know one, planning a family, losing virginity, getting shitfaced, turning on, toking up, getting one's nose opened, spending time in jail, growing up. In 1959 it means sticking, plunging, gouging into the chest, directly into the center of the upper torso with a sharp pointed object, wounded, bleeding, the pain at the point breaks through the bone structure into the cavity between the lungs, and the blood indicating life, growth, bright yellow and deep blue lights in the forebrain while the memory disintegrates and consciousness removes itself to the lower torso: pissing, shitting, farting, getting hard, everything being the same in this moment of most intense pain. 1959 means loss of innocence number 17. Contrast is everything and everything has changed.

He understands the decline of rock'n'roll by 1959. Payola, plastic, patriarchs, pimps. He turns to the detached, the aloof, the forbidden, jazz. 1956 getting off was "In the Still of the Night" and "Earth Angel." By 1960 it means *Milestones.* When Frankie Lyman and the Teenagers played Constitution Hall in Asbury Park, New Jersey, in the mid-fifties the riot that followed was racial by nature according to all newspaper accounts. There were no on-the-scene television reports. He watched several young white men chase a young black man down on the Asbury Park boardwalk, finally bringing him to his knees by flinging a baseball bat which caught him in the back. They beat him unmercifully. He wanted to love everyone by loving women, females, all kinds, all ages, like the Minsky advertisements in his own Newark. He wanted to love that black boy on the boardwalk by being romantic with his sister and offering whatever white sisters he might have in return. He vomited in the streets of Asbury Park. He attended Satanic nickel peep shows. The fat women in two-piece bathing suits that never showed anything but the folds of their asses when they turned around causing him to fall in love with that fold between buttocks and back of the thigh, wanting to rest his weary thirteen-year-old head there forever. Beating off under the boardwalk imagining things through the cracks between the long lean planks. Being bored with body surfing at last.

In 1956 the newspapers called it "rumbles" or gang wars, the gang people called it bopping, throwing hands, said: my man's got *heart*. Brave, jim. There was no room to go love love love in. There was little room to go touchy feely in. In the ocean of Belmar, New Jersey, fifteen-year-old Jewish girls from Lung Island allowed him and micks like him, and wops like him, and heinies like him, and polacks like him, and all kinds of cat licks like him, to explore beneath the tight one-piece styles of that summer. He knew what box meant. Believed in the mythology that said big box, good loving. Didn't know how or what for but knew had to. Stuck his finger in under the material and felt hair, opened his eyes underwater and saw hair, wanted to genuflect but there wasn't room.

You Remember Belmar NJ 1956

ethnic beaches. ethnic streets
ethnic hangouts, jetties, kids

got sand & their first glimpse
of hair where it never was

you piled into nosed & decked Chevies & Mercs
carried baseball bats to Bradley Beach to
beat up on Jews—You knew, they had all the
money & no restrictions on their sex like
Christians
           who said Hitler's only mistake was
           being born German but
           your own Jews rode with you:
           class warfare after all

Crazy Mixed Up Kids with names like
Sleepy, Face, Skippy, Skootch, Me Too Morrisey
& Nutsy McConnel imitated themselves & Marlon
Brando, danced to *Frankie Lyman & the Teenagers*
or *Little Richard* & sometimes
holding their fathers' guns
made women girls light their cigarettes trembling
letting them see just enough of it beneath their
pink or charcoal gray to make them happy or sick
always glad god made man out of dirt & not sand

you got drunk in your clubhouse or rented rooms
pretended you were really recording "In the Still of the
Night" or your own secret sleeper under
some name like the *Shrapnels* or the *Inserts* not
Spartans AC (Athletic Club) or the Archangels SC
(social ...

       the way we're still lining up

             (1967)

BADA-BING BADA-BRANDO

I was five years old in 1947, walking up my street, licking the inside of the top of a Dixie cup that contained a mix of vanilla and chocolate ice cream. The little round top had a tiny tab just big enough for my child fingers to grab and pull. You always licked the inside of the top before you used the little wooden peanut-shaped "spoon" that came with the cup. This was when, for a promotional gimmick, the inside of the tops had images of movie stars on them, in black and white, under a thin piece of foggy wax paper. So the drill was, first you licked the ice cream off the inside of the top, or more precisely off the thin piece of wax paper that separated it from the ice cream in the cup, and then you tried to guess who it was through the smoky paper.

This one time I knew instantly, and I almost broke my face from smiling so hard. I could see the famous blonde hair draped over one eye, with that sparkle in the other that implied a conspiracy between her and the viewer, like she was including you in on the joke of whatever it was that she found so secretly amusing about the whole experience of posing for a movie star photo. It was Veronica Lake of course, but not just her. Alan Ladd too. Both were my favorite movie stars at the time. It was a seminal moment. I pinned that little circle of Hollywood dreams—a dim and murky reproduction, after all, on the inside of a Dixie cup full of ice cream—on the slanted wall of the attic where I slept with my sisters, as my first secular icon.

∞

A few years later, I started having a recurring nightmare. It was too vague to understand or articulate, though I tried. I became more and more afraid of going to bed with no light on, but even more afraid of the light, because something about the lampshade, with little toy soldiers and teddy bears on it, and the way the light threw their silhouettes on the inside of my closed eyelids, kept nightmarish parades marching through my little head as I drifted off.

About that time, I was asked to play the theme from the movie *The Third Man* every time we visited anyone with a piano, or they visited us. It was this droning repetitive phrase played on some sort of Eastern European stringed instrument that you heard constantly on the radio that year. I would tinkle it out with my tiny hands on some relative's, or friend of my father's, piano, while everyone tried to look entertained and impressed.

It wasn't until I was standing in an auditorium at the University of Iowa in 1967 watching a student film society's screening of *The Third Man*—a movie I hardly remembered, except for the famous Ferris wheel scene and the rats in the sewer scene, though I didn't see any rats this time—that I made the connection. In that artfully subtle way old movies had of dealing with the deepest tragedies of life that movies now shove in your face with all their gory details, as Joseph Cotten's character visits the children's hospital to see the devastation that "Harry Lime's" greed has caused, we see no dying children, in fact, if I remember it correctly, we see no sick children at all, just their cribs and in the final image, a shot of an obviously much-loved teddy bear falling to the floor, the implication being that its tiny owner had just died.

It was that 1949 movie image that haunted my dreams when I was a child. And I never realized what it was or where it came from until two decades later.

∞

But it was in 1954 that I learned how to deal with my nightmares. In the original script for *On the Waterfront,* released that year, Terry Malloy, the character Marlon Brando plays, is introduced as a "jaunty waterfront hanger-on" in a "cap...whistling a familiar Irish song." Brando obviously made very different choices than the writer, Budd Schulberg. And not just because the actor studied for the role by hanging around the boxer Rocky Marciano, hardly a "jaunty Irish whistling" type, but because Brando and director Elia Kazan, as well as Schulberg, despite his Irish stereo-typing, were going for a kind of realism rarely seen before in American movies.

The film they ended up making had the look and feel of *Open City*, the Italian masterpiece of neo-realism that perfected the art of location shooting by filming an anti-Fascist movie in war-torn Rome while Nazi troops still patrolled the streets. The setting for *On the Waterfront* is just as real and vital to its storyline, if not as dangerous. Though there was some danger, and a need for police protection, in filming an exposé of mob-controlled unions on their own turf, on the Jersey side of the Hudson River, in Hoboken, at the time a hardworking, tough town full of the kind of longshoremen the movie was about.

There are unforgettable shots of these men, particularly toward the end, when Malloy has been beaten up and the dock-workers are waiting to see what he'll do. There's a long slow pan down a dock full of these guys that's like a gritty, grainy shot from some black-and-white 1930s union documentary.

Growing up not far from Hoboken, and not long after the movie came out being in a gang like the "Golden Warriors" of the film, the gang Malloy once led, it seemed like a documentary to me. The boys in that gang had haircuts and styles like ours, not like the Hollywood kid actors we usually saw in movies. They raised pigeons like us, and walked streets like ours, or close enough. The reality of the film was so deep and true that as a kid, I thought Brando was one of us, not a trained actor who grew up in Nebraska and went to a military school!

How could I believe otherwise? He talked like us, walked like us, was surrounded by guys who could have been our fathers or uncles or cousins or brothers. Some of them were. Like "Two Ton" Tony, a sometime professional boxer and wrestler well-known on our streets, who played one of Johnny Friendly's mob in the film. I remember as a kid seeing Two Ton's rotund figure in a bathing suit down the Jersey shore, where we all went in the sum-mer. He usually had a couple of young women—in what was as close to bikinis as they got back then—hanging from each arm as he strolled down the beach.

I wouldn't have believed Terry Malloy if Brando had, in fact, worn the cap and whistled the Irish tune and said the lines as writ-ten, instead of improvising based on the reality he was observing and absorbing and becoming a part of, the reality I knew so well.

Brando displayed his improvisational brilliance in one of his first lines, after unwittingly setting up his friend, Joey Doyle, for the mob guys to murder. Talking to Rod Steiger—who plays his brother Charlie—instead of the script's "I thought they were just going to talk to him," Brando says, "I thought they were just gonna lean on him a little."

That line alone was so memorable to me, so much the essence of what was most hip and creative about the people I was growing up around at the time and wanted so desperately to see portrayed truthfully in any medium, that I never forgot it, and used it myself a few times. How could Brando—this outsider from Nebraska and Broadway and Hollywood—and Schulberg—the quintessential Hollywood wunderkind—and Elia Kazan—the Broadway director—wealthy famous accomplished men of a world I had never known, nor had anyone I knew ever experienced even a hint of—how could these men manage to not only capture the reality we knew every day but turn it into an even deeper experience that enriched my understanding not only of my life and the lives around me, but of my desire for a life of the imagination that could still be true?

∞

It's almost too obvious that the source of the main story device— the Investigative Committee's need for witnesses to break the stronghold of the mob on the union—was the House Un-American Activities Committee hearings investigating the influence of the Communist Party in films, hearings that resulted in prominent Hollywood writers and directors going to prison, and many more losing their careers. Like actor John Garfield, who was "blacklisted" as a result of the hearings. Garfield was Schulberg's and Kazan's first choice to play Malloy, even though they both turned on their friends and "ratted" to the Committee. It's no coincidence that the lead character in *On the Waterfront* is put in a position that leaves him and the audience with only one choice to support: testifying.

After Malloy unwittingly sets up his friend Joey for the mob hit, he falls in love with Joey's sister Edie, played by Eva Marie Saint, in her Academy Award–winning screen debut. As if that isn't enough of an emotional turmoil to motivate his testifying, and it isn't, Schulberg has Charlie killed by order of Johnny Friendly, the same union boss Charlie worked for and protected with his legal counsel and skills. Friendly, played by Lee J. Cobb with a vengeance, adds a desperate realism that compels Malloy to take action against him. Cobb too was a "friendly" witness at the hearings that ruined so many Hollywood careers.

Despite the politics, and the stacked deck of a plot, Schulberg obviously had a deep desire to tell a real story. The inventiveness and dedication of Brando and Kazan made that desire a reality, and presented a challenge for everyone else involved. The studios initially turned Schulberg's idea down as too depressing, too different, too "real." But when Brando, the hottest young actor in Hollywood at the time, agreed to play the lead, the studios changed their minds. They still tried to destroy the integrity of the film by wanting it shot on studio back lots instead of on location, and in color.

On the Waterfront is one of the last great black-and-white films. The play of light and shadow is used almost as a way of scoring the nuances of the moral debate at the heart of the film, and of Terry Malloy's dilemma. The almost tragically innocent, yet not as delicate as she first seems, Edie is lit in a way that her fair hair and skin light up the bleak landscape of Hoboken. While Brando is often shot in shadows and semi-darkness. His acting complements the lighting so perfectly that even when he's with Saint in the glare of daylight, Brando comes across as still in the shadows. It is arguably Brando's greatest performance.

∞

By creating a "hero" who lives in a world where the only code he, or anyone he knew, has ever believed in forbids "ratting" of any kind, and then stacking the deck in favor of his doing just that, Schulberg and Kazan created for that time the ultimate "anti-hero." But Malloy's decision to testify is as heroic a stance as any of my favorite Western movie heroes of the time. He defies the sheep-like fear of the people of his world, to stand up alone, against their wishes, but as a living expression of their secret yearning, as he witnesses to the truth of their lives.

If that sounds close to a religious description of a spiritual experience, in the film it almost is. There were critics who compared Terry Malloy's fall and rise to the ordeal of Christ in his death and resurrection. Maybe it was just the extremes people went to, trying to justify something so politically volatile. But as a

Catholic kid with no knowledge of literary or film criticism, I sure saw the connection.

When Terry is beaten to a bloody pulp, as they used to say— and as I witnessed, and experienced, as a kid more than once— and is then encouraged by Karl Malden's Father Barry to "stand up," all by himself, not letting Edie or anyone else help him, and as the longshoremen watch, in that last great pan, as Brando stumbles and gets up and stumbles and gets up again, and forces himself, with unfocused blood-filled eyes to walk what seems to him, and us, like miles to the end of the dock, where the ship and the representative of its owners waits for these men to go to work, these men who refuse to do anything until they see what Terry does, until they see if he has the strength to lead them despite the beating he has taken, the strength to break the hold of the mobsters and thugs that have ruled their lives until now, when Brando so realistically—to me as a kid who had been beaten up badly myself at the time and had to get the strength to just make it home on my own, turning down requests from neighborhood women to help, or call for help—when Brando makes it, still standing, to the end of the dock, and the tall, well-dressed, anonymous representative of the powers that be yells, "Let's go to work," and the men pour in behind Terry as their new leader, until the iron gate comes down with a slam and "THE END" is superimposed on it, I felt like I had only felt before on Easter morning, when they pulled the purple coverings that hid the statues from sight during Lent and the stone figures seemed animated in their rediscovered visibility, and the altar boys gave up the muted wooden knocking instruments used since Ash Wednesday for the multiple bells they could now ring joyously, and the choir sang again with all their strength and devotion for the first time since Lent began. I felt it was like that, and in my heart I made the connection, without the help of any critic's searching for a metaphor to make a point.

∞

There were other moments in the film that were memorable. Some of them have become a part of our collective memories of images and lines that can conjure up entire eras, or summarize careers. The obvious one is Brando and Steiger in the back of the cab, when Charlie is about to set up his own brother, to be "leaned on" or worse. Terry laments, "I coulda been a contender," a line that a lot of us seem to know and have identified with.

We remember the tone, the inflection, the seemingly so true-to-life accent that will forever be associated with Brando saying, "You was my brother Charlie, you shoulda looked out for me." His hurt is so real to us that it's no surprise that Charlie finally does look out for him—and ends up "leaned on" himself, hanging dead on a fence from a longshoreman's baling hook, where Brando discovers him and tells Edie to stay with his dead brother while he goes after the murderers "and for god's sake don't leave him here alone."

There were also moments in the film—equally necessary and obvious and real—yet totally new in what they revealed at the time, and still do. Like when Terry finally testifies before the committee, "ratting" on Friendly. It is apparent even to Friendly in all his macho desperation that something is definitely finished, and it smells like his power. And then, the source of that power is revealed, in a simple and unique bit of storytelling, as we see the back of a seated old white man's head telling his butler to turn off the televised hearings, where Malloy has just testified. To the butler's, "Will that be all sir?" the man says, "If Johnny Friendly calls, we've gone out," and when the butler asks if that's for the day, the man answers that it is forever.

We've never seen or even heard of this man in the film before, nor do we ever see him again. But there is no forgetting his presence behind the power that was Johnny Friendly's. And it reduces the hearing room testimony of Brando's Malloy to a false resolution, a fake climax, because in reality there is always more to the story, and this movie is insistent in its dedication to reality. What happens after the little guy stands up to be counted, to be heard, to tell the truth? It's no surprise that after Terry testifies, he's rejected by the kids in the Golden Warriors who had looked up to him, by the friends who had made up the only company he kept, by the neighbors who may have dreamt of freedom from the Johnny Friendlys in their lives but nonetheless could not accept a "rat" in their midst. That was their, and my, reality. Brando plays Terry as if even he is disappointed in himself, but only because testifying against Friendly isn't enough of a revenge for Charlie's death. He has to do something more real, for that time and place.

And he does. He goes back to the docks to take out his anger and vengeance on Johnny Friendly's skull, to call him out, to challenge him to this "Eastern's" version of the then so popular

Western's climactic shoot-out. But unlike the typical Western that glorified a kind of instant but almost bloodless showdown, the knock-down, drag-out fight that is the climax of *On the Waterfront* is as real as they got back then. A man standing up to a bully gets beaten to a pulp by that bully and his henchmen. No Western would have survived such an ending, nor any Hollywood film of the time. Nor would *On the Waterfront.* Maybe that's why it didn't stop there, but continued the struggle in that walk to freedom, so memorable it seems like actual history is taking place and not just a movie being made.

And maybe history *was* being made, at least movie history, but more than the Oscars for Best Picture and Best Actor and Best Supporting Actor and Best Screenplay and all the rest. Maybe this was a turning point for the movies, the place where the later triumphs of the American cinema of the 1960s and '70s, when such "realists" as Martin Scorcese and Francis Ford Coppola (as operatic as his "realism" can be) changed the Hollywood formula movie into something more recognizable as real life, and real art, maybe this is the point where that kind of American moviemaking began.

It certainly was in my heart, as Father Barry encouraged Terry to "stand up," even though he can hardly see through his blood-soaked eyes or stand on his wobbly punchdrunk legs—to "stand up" and lead these actors and actual dockworkers to the ship that lies waiting for someone to unload, to lead these men who are waiting to see if he can. What moment can match the power of that stumbling falling struggle to walk alone up that gangplank from boss Friendly's houseboat office and through the men who make a path for him and down that endless dock to where the representative of the ship's owners, the power on the other side, is waiting for men to come to work, whoever is leading them.

And when he makes it—when he made it—I knew there was a chance I might make it too. Not in a typical Hollywood fantasy way of "happily ever after," but in the reality-based way of my life and experience at that time. The reality of getting up after getting your ass kicked, no matter how many people were against you or abandoned you or let you down, standing up for yourself and your own truth and seeing it through to the end, no matter what might happen.

TO BE ALONE

To be alone and not talk much,
that was the way to get the women.
To be alone and talk too much
was the way to get yourself a
reputation as a jerkoff, a big
mouth, a noise, unless you made
it your noise so uniquely you
became a freak, so personally
you became impossible to ignore
or learn from, so honest and
unrelenting and smart you became
a fucking legend in your own
town, your own home, your own
place to be alone because it
didn't change that much even
when you were invited to parties
to be a conversation piece, a
possible save in case it didn't
turn out too lively, got boring
and people needed something to
distract them from the ways
they couldn't be together.
You could name those ways and
demonstrate them, and sometimes,
more and more often as you got
better and better at your noise,
the ladies with their own noisy

struggles with their own excited
souls and peculiarities gave you
what the others got by keeping
quiet from the women who were
in between, because the quiet
ones came to your noise too,
only not when anyone else was
noticing, just for you, just to
hear you tell them what they
meant to hear by being quiet
but the others didn't know—
until you knew so much about
them, there was nothing left
but to be cool too and turn it
into something else like
music or dope or poetry ...

It seems so fucking stupid to complain.

Who's Sorry Now?

That was a song from the 1920s. Connie Francis recorded it in the '50s to please her father and it made her a star. She's from New Jersey. I'm from Jersey too. Are you from Jersey? I hated that bit Joe Pepsico, or whatever his name is, used to do on *Saturday Night Live* during its lamest seasons. There's good reasons why I left New Jersey, but I still can be proud of what I left behind.

I always thought *Strangers on a Train* was Hitchcock's best film, not just for the murder reflected in the victim's fallen glasses, or the out-of-control carousel—or because Robert Walker was so pre-Dean compelling in this totally underplayed and played-out way—or all the other reasons, but because South Orange, where I grew up, was mentioned in the first moments of the film.

I went to Our Lady of Sorrows grammar school with the girl whose father cared for the grounds of the tennis club, where we all believed the tennis match in that movie was shot. Later on I worked with her big brother, who was the toughest and coolest looking Irish dude we knew.

He left long before I did. I was only a kid, but because we worked together he let me hang with him and some other aspiring tough guys. One night we all went to the town next door in his old Chrysler, a kind of classic from the '40s that at that time was just considered old, but he kept in great shape and it was a cool machine to be seen in as we pulled up to the birthday party of this Italian girl from Orange he was seeing.

The family treated us warmly, but there was some suspicion in the air at this little gang of Irish dudes. Butch, that was his name, was the biggest person there, with his pink Irish smiling cherub face and flattop haircut and muscled body underneath the white tee shirts we all wore. He stood out like some future president or union leader or hero cop.

But sometime before the party was supposed to stop, he came and got us. Seems someone warned him it was time to leave. He looked mad as hell as we walked out ready to do some damage, until we got to his car. What was left of it. I thought he was gonna cry or kill somebody, but all he did was stare and stare as if his eyes could undo the damage they saw there, but they couldn't because there was too much.

Every inch of the body had been smashed. The windows and headlights and anything glass had all but disappeared into such tiny pieces, it looked like maybe it had rained where they had fallen into pools of sparkling reflections of the streetlights overhead. All four tires were slashed to shreds, like some kind of rubber black confetti celebrating the death of something.

Maybe that beautiful old Chrysler body, because it certainly had passed into some other life, no longer the one we were still in, as we all stood there and tried to find a pin-size spot that could remind us of what this car had once been. But there were none. The complete machine had been undone, as if some giant hand had crushed it like a piece of paper, where a poem was once begun and then abandoned.

Which is what we did. Without a word, we just started moving like some dumb and frightened-into-submission herd of our lower selves. We walked all the way back to our homes, without any goodbyes, and no one ever saw Butchy again. His sister said he joined the Navy the next day and was gone within hours.

I lasted a few more years, until I was almost as old as Butchy when he disappeared. Only I joined the Air Force, 'cause the recruiter convinced me I could go on playing jazz in an officers' club in Manhattan, once I got through basic training, which of course wasn't true. And I didn't leave because someone smashed up my car. I didn't have a car until a few years later, and I did all the smashing up whenever I drove drunk, which was all the time.

But I did leave because of a girl. I think I thought I was gonna make her sorry for something she had done that I don't remember anymore. I wonder if she's ever sorry for whatever it was.

Is As

It's time for beauty
to make its return—
not anorexic girls in
post-heroin mode—not
middle-class children of
divorce pretending to be
death until they are—
not aging babies crying
for their milk & honey—
not "not"—any of it—
just sit & wonder, awed—
owed the comfort of an
eye in sight of itself—
this is a fact, beauty
doesn't ache, it reverberates
inside our consciousness of
bliss—I can't believe I just
said that—"Rip don't!"—
"Nardo—Nar—*doe*"—"Aghhh!"
What I mean here is De-
liverance—from all that is
so boringly appalling about
fate—a turning on to all that
is inspiringly appealing about
hate for the nondescript of—
make a list—your own—of
what you'd want to hear on

the phone—see in the mirror
out the window of your car—
another world—the one we're
in—kiss me—touch my hair—
anywhere—show me the cover
of a book that is as beautiful
as we all once were—be.

SIDE STORY

1

In 1955 I became a teenager. That same year the movie that changed my life, and the lives of all my friends, came out: *Blackboard Jungle*. When the military marching drumbeat under the opening credits turns into the rock'n'roll of Bill Haley's "Rock Around the Clock," the first rock'n'roll to be heard coming from a movie screen (unlike *Rebel Without a Cause* which came out the same year but had some kind of easy listening sound coming from Dean's car radio, not to mention the geeky, to us Jersey boys, Southern California version of cool), the movie theater erupted. And no amount of cops could put the genie back in the bottle.

The very next day, even kids who liked Eddie Fisher singing "Oh My Papa" or Patti Page's "Tennessee Waltz" were walking around calling everyone "Daddy-o." Within days several gangs had formed. There was one poor aging Italian immigrant kid, sixteen and still in grammar school, who had made up his own gang jacket, writing on the back of the one he'd worn every day to school for years: "15 Daredevils." Kids laughed at him behind his back, sometimes to his face. But I thought to myself, who knows, maybe he is in some kind of gang called "15 Daredevils."

There already was an Italian gang called the "Pink Devils." They went so far as to have tiny homemade crucifix tattoos between the forefingers and thumbs of their right hands. But the gang I joined was all Irish. Irish-American I suppose they'd say now. But back then, when fights between Italian-American gangs and Irish-American gangs were called "race wars" in the Newark

71

newspapers, hyphenates were unknown. We were just Irish or Italian or Polish or Jewish or Negro or whatever.

The biggest gangs were in the nearby cities. Newark had the Romans, an Italian gang supposedly several hundred strong. They were rumored to use butcher knives in "rumbles" and were feared throughout Northern New Jersey. The largest Irish gang was called the Loafers, from Jersey City. Three hundred strong and from thirteen to twenty-one. They were rumored to have an initiation rite that included being dropped off in a "colored" neighborhood with nothing but a baseball bat, and you had to come back alive.

But in our little town—a nineteenth-century suburb of Newark, with a lot of wealth and a little lower-class immigrant working poor who served the needs of that wealth—we only had about a dozen members in the Spartans. By the time we got our customized red jackets with white shoulder inserts, we had to add A.C. under the name, for "Athletic Club," because the authorities had outlawed gangs by then. To get around the ban, gangs added "A.C." or "S.C." for athletic or social club.

Most of the kids in it were from middle-class families who had been in this country longer than mine. In fact, I wasn't included in the original plans when the gang formed. I had a huge paper route at the time that I bought off two classmates who had split it between them. Most kids worked off a truck for the guy who had the local franchise for news delivery. But those kids made only about three dollars a week. By running my own route I could make up to sixteen.

I was going to buy the route with a guy from my neighborhood, but my father was going through a painful business loss at the time, due to a partner he felt doublecrossed him, so he refused to let me buy into any business, no matter how small, with any partner. It was a terrible burden for a kid with a bike to cover the several miles the route encompassed. So my first task was to cut it down, by convincing people close to home to take a subscription with me, rather than the truck guy. I promised I'd leave the paper at their door, not on their roof or lawn or sidewalk or wherever.

It worked. And as I gradually added subscribers closer to home, I'd let go those furthest away. Before I got it down to a manageable area, I had a younger cousin who lived next door help me out on days when other activities cut into delivery time. On one of those days, he delivered to the home of a classmate who was one of nine kids and lived in a big house on the other side of town. There, my cousin overheard this crewcut, redheaded Irish kid talking about forming the Spartans.

My cousin brought the news home to me, and when I confronted my classmate the next day at school, he—reluctantly I realize now, and must have known then but repressed—agreed to let me in. We all had our names inscribed with white thread over our hearts on the front of the jackets. When we got them and first put them on, it was like nothing before. I was in a gang. Officially. For all the world to see. At a time when teenager and juvenile delinquent were almost interchangeable, I entered both wearing a bright red jacket with white shoulder inserts and white lettering: "Mike" scripted across my heart and "SPARTANS A.C." across the back.

We were seventh graders at the time, but soon would be eighth graders, top of the heap, and we felt already cooler than those older guys who hadn't gotten it together fast enough to have jackets for their gangs before they graduated and split up to go to various high schools. We knew we ruled and so did everyone else. It was exhilarating.

That summer, down the Jersey shore where I went every year to stay in a "bungalow" my grandmother owned, the crippled one who lived with us, I wore the jacket even in the heat. Until one evening I was bopping down the boardwalk with a friend, who wasn't in any gangs but was proud to be accompanying me, the gangster, on my tour of the scene. I found myself suddenly surrounded by a bunch of really big and scary Italian guys from Newark in red and white gang jackets of their own.

Thank God they weren't Romans. Their jackets said "Indians," and they scared the shit out of me for a while, threatening me, spinning me around so they could each get a shot at me. I was wearing a man's hat, with the front and back sewed up, à la Leo Gorcey and the old Bowery Boys films I loved, with, if I remember this correctly, charms sewn onto the brim, but what I thought were cool charms, not like the ones my sisters wore on their little bracelets, these were tiny guns and handcuffs and like that.

The Indians couldn't figure me out. I was much younger and smaller than these city boys in their late teens. But I was kind of gutsy, out of fear, I now know, but nonetheless, I acted like a tough little gangster and they weren't sure if there were any more of me around or this was it. So they roughed me up a little, teased me a lot, and then decided I was all right and let me go with a warning not to wear my jacket anymore that summer because they were running Belmar that year.

When I got back to school in the Fall, things deteriorated even more. I fractured my thumb in a football game we played against some other gang. But since injuries were thought of as weaknesses in my house, I tried to hide it at dinner that night, avoiding lifting anything with that hand. The next day in school the teacher saw my swollen thumb and sent me to the nurse who sent me to the doctor, who lived a few doors away from the school and usually came to our house when we needed him. He took x-rays, saw it was fractured and put a cast on it.

That night at the dinner table the only brother still at home made fun of me for needing a cast. I knew he was tough because not only was he a cop, but when he got drafted he had these rotten black teeth that the Army pulled out and told my mother had been infected, probably for years, and must have been so painful it was a wonder he hadn't cried every time he ate. But he hadn't even seemed to notice it.

The fracture took me away from the games, and I needed help delivering my papers. The youngest of the ten kids in the family on the other side of us, a few years younger than me, helped me out for free. I'd buy him sodas and candy and teach him the tough guy stuff I thought I was learning. The guys in the gang called him "slave Ray" because he seemed to do whatever I told him to, and made jokes I didn't quite get about him and me and our neighborhood.

They all came from the other side of town, which seemed more "middle-class" and "American" to us, though it was full of the same kinds of ethnic groups, just in America for more generations. And their fathers finished high school. Most had college degrees and worked in a "profession." My father dropped out of school after the seventh grade to go to work. He'd made some money and started and lost a few businesses, but he was intimidated by rich people, even middle-class people, and was kind of a character who played the ponies every day and made a little book on the side, and at this time was struggling financially after losing another business.

I seemed to spend less and less time with the Spartans, and they began to make me the butt of their jokes more and more, using my short temper as entertainment when they were bored, goading me into rages I couldn't seem to control. Especially after my cast came off. Until one day, one of them pushed me so far I went ballistic, and they decided to teach me a lesson.

We were down at the Community House, where we played basketball or shot pool. There was an indoor gym we were using, and they got me down and rolled me up in a gym mat with only my head sticking out. Then they took basketballs and played a game of seeing who could come closest to my head without hitting me. Of course, they often missed.

Eventually, they starting feeling bad about it and stopped, unrolled the mat and let me out. I told them I quit their stupid gang, and they said they were going to kick me out anyway. When I got outside the tires on my bike had been punctured and I had to walk it the mile and a half home.

I eventually got my revenge. I challenged each of them, one at a time, to fight me after school, and half of them chickened out. The others fought me to a draw. I wasn't a very good fighter, but I had endurance. I wouldn't quit. So eventually they'd suggest we stop. It actually got me closer to a few of them, and made me see through the rest of them for the elitist phonies they were. But it also left me without a gang.

That summer down the shore, I hung around some of the "Indians" and ended up being the liaison for a rumble on the beach one night between the Italians and the Jews. The Jews were mostly from New York and weren't pushovers like a lot of the ones I knew from my hometown. The Italians were gonna kill them though, with sharpened studs on their garrison belts and sharpened car antennas as whips, because the rules said no knives or zip guns.

But the rumble never happened. Me and the leader of the Jewish gang were arrested as the instigators before it even began. I felt very cool being hauled away from the penny arcade where all the kids hung out, police siren wailing and all. But the cops didn't like my attitude and quickly reduced me to near tears when they beat the backs of my thighs with their billy clubs because I was taking too long to walk from their patrol car to the station house.

My father looked like he had a heart attack when they brought me home after I used his best friend, the chief of police back home, as someone they could parole me to. It was a mess. I had entered a new phase, beyond playing, into real bad boy territory, where girls were told to stay away from me and local thugs looked at me with new eyes.

Among the girls who actually admired my "police record" was a tough Italian girl from Newark who hinted she was from a mob-connected family. She was dark-skinned and dark-eyed and dark-haired and though I was too busy with a redheaded Irish girl with enormous breasts that summer, me and this Italian girl made some kind of connection.

In the Fall, now a high school freshman, I crashed a party in a neighboring town, with some guys from my neighborhood. It was in a house on the hill, one of the new '50s style ranch houses we all secretly wished we lived in. The party was in the basement "rec room." The kids were all "rich" to us. When we showed up the girl threatened to have us thrown out, but we knew nobody would actually challenge us.

Then she said, "The Archangels will be here soon and then you'll be sorry." We actually got a little worried. But when this gang we hadn't heard of showed up, they turned out to be regular, in fact, exceptionally nice guys, and the party continued with no problems. That's when I saw the Italian girl from Newark.

It turned out she'd been lying about coming from Newark. Except in the sense that all of us had come from there, or our families before we were born. She lived in a house on the hill, and her family was often away while she stayed alone with the live-in maid. She was an only child. She told me all this in the back seat of a 1955 Chevy one of my neighborhood pals had borrowed from his father. As we made out. And eventually went close enough to all the way to have me reach a climax but without worrying about pregnancy.

I felt terrible. Like she had tricked me. I had been into a newfound control of my sexual urges and now here I was back in a sinful state again. And besides, she had hair on her nipples which I hadn't even known was possible for a girl and embarrassed me not only for her, but for me, since I didn't have any on my chest yet at all. I swore I'd never see her again. But the first time she called I arranged to go visit her.

I had a friend from an Irish family of fifteen who lived around the corner and had an old pickup truck. He'd dropped out of high school so my father didn't like me hanging around with him. He was older, obviously, since he drove, and tried to look even older, by dressing like the old guys, in slacks and baggy shirt, and was always flashing a roll of money he made working construction.

I talked him into driving me over to this girl's house on the hill in the next town. He was supposed to hang out with the maid while the Italian girl and I got it on. But on entering her home, we had to cover for our awkwardness, intimidated by the wealth of what was just a normal middle-class home without a million kids and immigrant grandparents and the rest of our experience. Her parents were away again. And she'd given the maid the night off so we could be alone.

This girl was a showoff and started bragging about the things she got to do because her parents were rich. Among trips to Florida and various islands and other stuff my friend found impressive, she mentioned Broadway plays. I had never been to a Broadway play, but I had loved my trips to Manhattan with my family, to see movies at Radio City Music Hall and light candles at St. Patrick's Cathedral and wander Times Square looking up at the lights and billboards, like the one with the man blowing smoke rings advertising Camel cigarettes.

Broadway had a resonance for me in a way I had repressed, because it would have been called "faggy." So I let my friend make some dumb jokes about that, and acted as if I too was ready to put it down. She defended "the theater" by jumping up—we were in some sort of entertainment room, with a bar, which we were drinking profusely from, and a TV and a hi-fi record player—and putting on the brand new cast album from the musical *West Side Story*.

I couldn't believe my ears. Were these people singing, "Officer Krupke, fuck you!" They weren't, of course, they were singing, "Krup you," but it sounded like "Fuck you" at a time when Norman Mailer had invented the word "fug" to get around the censorship of those days. I was stunned at the audacity and nerve of it. As well as by the words that preceded it about little gang kids and the reasons we did what we did.

I had already become a part of the Archangels, which mostly meant hanging around their clubhouse in a converted garage in West Orange, down in the valley near the tracks, like where we lived. I found it fascinating that the gang was made up of Italians and Irish and Polish and even some guys that seemed like old time Americans.

They were amazingly easy going. They rode around—when not reading girlie magazines or playing the pinball machines the Italian member supplied through an uncle in "the vending machine business"—in the oldest member's car. He worked in a decal shop and had made one up to put on the back of his pre-war coupe that said "TEENAGE DRIVER AND PROUD OF IT."

I loved cruising with those guys, because they had no evil intentions. All they wanted to do was take it easy, maybe pick up some girls, crash a party on the hill, smoke some cigarettes, drink some beer, read girlie or car magazines, play some pinball and avoid hassles as much as possible. As far away as we were from the gangs in *West Side Story,* I could still identify with the sentiments expressed in Stephen Sondheim's lyrics. I was captivated. To the point I ignored the Italian girl so I could play the record again and listen more closely—supposedly to decipher if they were or were not really saying "fuck you."

After a few failed attempts at getting my interest back, she disappeared with my friend and I ended up memorizing the lyrics to every song on the album. I never saw her again. My friend started his own construction company, and my father went from being angry at me for hanging out with him to being angry at me for not having his ambition and work ethic. The Romeo and Juliet story behind that album I was unaware of, but it entered my consciousness, and because one of the differences between me and the Spartans that had rejected me was my burgeoning love of black music not as something to laugh at and make jokes at the expense of but to admire, I found myself noticing the few black girls in our neighborhood more and more. The Archangels didn't seem to notice, or mind, as I drifted away from them and started hanging out more and more with the "colored" guys. And girls.

2
....

When the movie of *West Side Story* finally came out, I was stationed in South Carolina in the Air Force. I had already been court-martialed, and had had many article fifteens, which is the disciplinary action short of a court-martial. And I had rejected white culture entirely and adapted the manner and style and speech of the black musicians I played with and emulated.

I also had fallen in love with a beautiful black girl from Atlantic City I met in a Greenwich Village bar shortly after she moved there after graduating from high school. She was dark and thin and had the most beautiful eyes I'd ever seen. But my parents objected when we got engaged, and so did hers, and she jumped into the bohemian pre-hippie scene enthusiastically, which left me jealous of her Village friends and imagined and real lovers.

In fact I joined the service to get away from my broken heart. Now she was pregnant. It had happened while I was in basic training. Some guy she met briefly at a party while back in Atlantic City. But she never told him and didn't love him and still said she loved me, as I still did her. We were still too young to get married without parental consent, neither of us twenty-one yet. Her father still wanted to shoot me and threatened to do so if I ever showed up at his door where she was back staying in her delicate condition.

We talked to each other regularly on the phone and tried to work out a compromise where she would give the child up to a foster home until we saw if we were going to really get married and then we'd get it back and raise it with our own. It was all very romantically rebellious and us against them and Romeo and Juliet and *West Side Story*. So when the movie came out and played at the base theater, I convinced my black buddies we had to go see it.

Needless to say, musicals weren't exactly respected in this place. But I got emotionally involved in the story. The songs already meant so much to me, I performed most of them in the little jazz trios and other groups I'd played piano in for years. So when the audience of enlisted men and their girlfriends and wives started making loud jokes at the expense of those on the screen I stood up in the dark and turned to yell at them: "It's a fucking musical! If you don't wanna see singing and dancing get the fuck out, or shut the fuck up!"

I already had a reputation for being crazy. And since this was South Carolina at a time when everything outside the base was still segregated, to the point that a black man couldn't go to the drive-in movie in his own car, and even on the base it was voluntarily segregated, the dances, the mess hall, etc., and I was always with the black dudes, some of whom resented me for my "race" and some of whom got a kick out of me or used me for their own ends, and some of whom genuinely were my friends, and the white dudes just made jokes at me but not where I could hear them, somehow, it worked. The audience stayed quiet for the rest of the film.

Once outside, my black friends started making fun of it, pretending to dance, leaping across the base mock-singing "Tonight," etc. It made me laugh, which I needed, because I really wanted to cry, thinking about my love and our screwed-up lives and chances at happiness. The next night when I called her she was upset and sounded as though she needed rescuing.

I called my family after I hung up from telling her I would take a leave and come see her and maybe we'd finally get married. I asked my father again for his permission, a legal necessity, and he blew up on me again. This time he said I was out of the family for good, my name would never be spoken again, etc., etc.

I left the next morning, hitchhiking up the East Coast. I got picked up by a truckdriver who took me a long way. I told him about my girl being black, and the redneck white trash high school dropout Southern white man told me to go for it. Like a lot of people I knew, he didn't fit the stereotype. At least not alone with him in the cab of his truck.

After him I got picked up by two teenage white girls who took me to a roadside restaurant dance club once it got dark and when one of them started crawling all over me on the dance floor the management kicked us out. We were drunk by then, and they took turns screwing me in the back of their car. One of them ripped the back of my shirt with her nails, drawing blood even. They were passionate girls. And, it turned out, both divorced already at seventeen.

They dropped me off at a motel in Winston-Salem where my father was staying on his way to play the ponies for a week, as he did every winter, in Florida. He was alone. My mother had reached me before I left, convincing me to stop and see him. I arrived drunk, and as a recovering alcoholic I knew this pissed him off. I didn't realize that it also hurt him to see me that way.

He yelled but I fell asleep before he finished. In the morning we had breakfast, and he harangued me about the dangers for the children of a mixed marriage and his old bromide about how you started marriage with one strike against you just because you were two different genders, and if the woman wasn't Irish that was strike two, if not Catholic, strike three. But I assured him she was Catholic, so we had one strike still to go.

He didn't find it funny. He took back my banishment from the family but still wouldn't consent to our marriage. He also made some snide comments about having seen the condition of my shirt when I passed out the night before. It wasn't anything new. I often came home, when I still lived there, with torn clothes and blood on me, usually from fights. But he had figured this one out with no problem.

It was strange that I felt no guilt over the girls in the car. It seemed natural to me. As it did to my black girlfriend. The bohemianism we embraced in the Village and beyond, included a kind of "free love" that predated the hippies. We knew we loved each other, it was just a matter of how far we were willing to go to be married and make a family together.

The movie of *West Side Story* had me all googoo-eyed about our chances. So the first thing I did after checking into some dump little rundown hotel in an Atlantic City that was dying, pre-casino days this was, and then hooking up with her was to take her to the movies to see it. Afterward, as I was holding the door open for her and her big belly, moved even more this time by what I now thought of as "our story," she dismissed my romanticism with a cutting remark about how "Life is no movie."

She was still a teenager. I was barely twenty. She was several months pregnant by a man she didn't love and in love with a crazy romantic white boy who wanted to live out a movie fantasy. I left the hotel to stay in a house some friends of hers used as a crash pad, though that term hadn't been coined yet. They were all black kids who had been basically abandoned by their families. One of them had lost his parents in an accident and gotten the house as a result.

They grudgingly let me sleep there and hang out when my girl was with her parents, trying to get them to give in. Her mother was more than willing, but her father was still determined that no white boy would ever be a part of his family. Finally, her father agreed to meet with me at the home of one of her aunts. He promised he wouldn't bring his pistol.

I bought a bottle of bourbon, a fifth in fact. I waited in an upstairs room nervously, until his arrival. He was brought in by my girl and then she left for us to talk. We sat across the room from each other in straight-back chairs in silence for a few minutes while he glared at me. He was short, but formidable. All muscle and rage. It obviously came from hard work and the oppression he'd been through because of the deep blackness of his skin. I knew enough to know that he was on the lowest rung of the color hierarchy and knew it and resented it with everything in him.

I don't remember exactly how I started, but I'm sure it included offering him a drink from the bottle I was drinking from. In those days, I knew from my experiences in the South, that drinking from the same bottle broke a lot of years of resentment with some black men, since few white men were willing back then to share spit with non-whites.

After a few swigs each, we both loosened up and he began to tell me why he hated me and my kind and my race and my history and all the rest. I came back, after letting him vent, with some of my own agreement about my race, and even my family, but pointed out that when his people were slaves, mine were starving to death with grass stains on their lips, in their own country. You know the story. Or should.

I also pointed out that in my experience, whites and blacks both included a lot of assholes and pretentious jerks. He almost cracked a smile at that. By the time we finished the bottle, he was warming up, and yelled down for his wife or daughter or someone to bring us another. They did. And we polished off that. By the time we finished a third, he was advising me that I was an idiot for wanting to marry his daughter when she was dumb enough to get knocked up by someone else. Let the other dude pay the price, was his advice.

I didn't take it. I told him I loved her and didn't give a shit what anyone thought. He seemed to admire that. When his daughter and wife and sister-in-law came up finally to see what the decision was, he told them I was the first white person he ever liked, and if we two fools wanted to get married, he wouldn't stand in the way.

She had already spoken to the priest at her church and he was willing to marry us without the legalities. The church rules allowed marriages as young as thirteen, or so we heard. Especially if the girl was pregnant. So even though legally, according to the government, we wouldn't be married and get the benefits of the married servicemen and all that, we'd be married in the eyes of the church.

But when we showed up to talk to the priest about the wedding, he had left town for a sudden vacation. In his place was an Irish priest from the old country, a young one, who tried to explain why he couldn't do it and make it sound like it wasn't fear of reprisal from whoever had intimidated her priest into leaving town.

She decided the answer was to become Jewish. I got pissed off at the ludicrousness of that, and at her anti-Irish remarks about the priest. We argued, I returned to South Carolina, where my locker and the little cubicle I slept in had been completely stripped bare. My favorite clothes, and cheap little mono record player and books and art and everything I owned. All gone. The white guys in the barracks said, "Gee, we saw these colored boys taking your stuff and figured they must be friends of yours you were letting use it while you were away."

We got together a few more times, including when she had the baby. I was there in the hospital in Newark with her, where everyone assumed I was the father. But eventually we drifted apart. She got the baby back from the foster home anyway, and ended up marrying a third guy. I got married too. To a woman I hardly knew. But that's another story. We had two kids, and my first true love had a few more too. Like me, she married more than once. We remain good friends and my love has never diminished. For her, or for *West Side Story.*

NOTHING

Nothing in his experience could compare to the way he felt when he was part of a crowd of three hundred or even three thousand or more in control of a city street or park, legally sanctioned or not, it didn't matter what stance any authorities took, they were in charge of that space in ways he had never experienced anywhere else or any other time, it was 1969 and when there was a real "demonstration," not just some futile exercise in speech-making little different from some straight political rally or even the May Day ceremonies when he was a kid and all the Catholic school children would march to the local park from the church, the few special girls in front in their bright pastel dresses, or all in white, scattering flowers before the statue of the Blessed Virgin that a few special boys carried to the spot in the park where there was a stage set up for the priests and a few local dignitaries to talk at them about the evils of Communism and the virtues of Catholic Americans (with an unstated prejudice in favor of Irish Catholic Americans since that was what he and his family were and most of the kids and all the priests). There was nothing like the exhilaration of being in a crowd of people who shared the same purpose, the same need to let the rest of the world know them in that way, to see them and hear them and understand that there was nothing they could do short of killing them all that would stop this movement against the stupidity of the war and of the still all-pervasive racism and most of all against the ridiculous barrenness of the legacy of the fifties—the sterility and banality and deadening conformity that had dominated the society and culture for so long. They were protesting that, the atomizing depersonalizing regimentation of a time when only the radio and a few parties could make you feel a part of something more vital, something more meaningful *to you* and the people you were sure were like you out there somewhere but not reflected in their boring media or culture. Now here they were, the fellow humans you were sure *were* your "brothers and sisters" like the blacks put it and the union organizers and activists put it and the Southern fundamentalists and secret sects put it, your brothers and sisters totally taking over a street where no car could go now, no others interested only in their own security and petty little schemes to avoid trouble and notice in a world where until you and those like you that had been the controlling factor, the fear of detection, of being singled out as the loony, the commie, the freak, the enemy, now you were all making it clear, *you were* freaks and commies and crazies and the fucking enemy and you didn't care, you were even proud of it, because where else could you feel so strong and brave and energized and happy and free. The only thing that compared with it was the overwhelming tenderness and pride you felt when you looked around at a peaceful demonstration on a sunny afternoon in a pleasant park or campus and saw how beautiful so many of your fellow freaks were, their long flowing hair and crazy bushes extending from their heads like sensuous antennae into the surrounding atmosphere, making it crackle with the possibilities of a sexuality that included the beauty of the basic elements, like hair, and skin, so much bare skin among the crazy patterns and colors, the clothes as much like some sort of sexual advertising as anything, everyone looking soft and almost androgynous in their common styles but individually distinct in their variations on the extraordinary combinations that this society hadn't seen since the Wild West or the most outrageously got-up Rodeo Indians or the dreams of Teenage America growing up in the desolate Fifties on the promise of rock'n'roll.

SUPERREALISM

First of all I'm naked
while I'm typing this,
only my rash is airbrushed,
the rest is visceral energy
for my poetry, in this case
depicted objects of tough-minded
harsh light that emphasizes
the previous generation of
dismayed bridegrooms at the
altar of the cosmic alienation.

I mean for instance me,
and Winch, and our contemporaries
were tuned up by neosurrealist
poets, trite poets, hardnosed
rugged individualist poets and
ironic pap poets of the '50s and '60s.
We apply the new techniques,
along with a thorough knowledge
of consumer products that share
the airless synergetic crackle
of methodologies, to our experiences
like cosmetics in the undertaker's
steady but too subjective grip.

Actually I'm cold sitting here
at the typewriter on my lunch hour

naked and exhausted from masturbating
all morning to create the right mood
for poetry uninvolved in the ego
like the "actualist poetry" of the
early '70s with which I was associated
without my foreknowledge or permission
or agreement or even knowing what was
meant by that term. It had something
to do with the reproduction of
objects in "the poem" as though
they were "actual" not *transcendy*!

In some poetry circles craftsmanship is
considered to be a dazzling array of
chromatic effects that draw our attention
like a physical presence, but to us
superrealists on the nonhierarchical
ladder of self esteem the elusiveness of
technique in a savage amalgam of clarity
avoids value judgments as to what ought
to be deceptive or enthusiastic toward
the unimaginative and divides the universe
into something spilled and something
wiped up. This is one example.

THE SEVENTIES

It's all so romantic. I'm so romantic. I can fantasize some sweet starlet's ass in front of my eyes, so round and soft and delicious until I want to cry or masturbate or have her fart in my face and then ten seconds later a sad song will have me yearning for a Ginger Rogers–Fred Astaire innocence I can't remember ever having but know I lost anyway.

Life ain't just hanging out waiting to be discovered and I've been as busy as anybody the past 32 years but somehow I still feel like I'm hanging out. We called it "hackin aroun" in the '50s. Those terrible years when only the Italians seemed to really look the role, laughing at older people and hicks and general non-hip people taking Brando and Dean for one of them. Shit. Maybe in Hollywood thugs looked like that, but any rebels we knew looked absolutely flawless and tough and only sensitive to the brother feeling. Don't fuck with their brothers, the romance in their eyes when they could see their own kind hurting. They had more than one heart jim.

Music kept it going then and still does. But we can't hold a tune, above our heads, sang Johnny Ray and someone. "Up Above Our Heads, There's Music in the Air" and then it's gone, said Eric Dolphy. Gone, that's what we said instead of "Bad" or "Boss" or "Dynamite" or "Far Out" or "Right On" or hey that's a little bit of all right. Well all right. And it ends like everything else ends, in the faces of some stranger.

I don't think we know how to live like failures anymore.

(11-24-74)

Sonnet for My 33rd

Brigitte Bardot
Abbott & Costello
Hound Dog
The Dickey Bird Song
The Girl Can't Help It
T. S. Eliot
Cassius Clay
JFK
Thelonius Sphere Monk
On the Waterfront
Bird
Pope John XXIII
Ezra Pound
Clifford Brown

from HARDWORK

do it now
though there can be no name
for "it"

∞

"Frank O'Hara is the
Fred Astaire of American Poetry"
whispers Bruce Andrews during
That's Entertainment, Part II

I wanted to be the Frank Sinatra

∞

I thought the Garden of Eden a
metaphor for pubic hair—I meant
the garden I wanted to give
—I couldn't help what it was
there—at 34 I don't think too much
about death but it's there as a
comfort to the living—
—despite the fun—and
joy!—in the twist of the torso
perfecting its fall—o my god how
I thank you for all the bodies—
the gardens—

what's there—

∞

"It's a mistake to say 'He looks so
young'—Why not say that's the
way some people look when they're
old?"
                    —Gale Sondegaard
                    V.V. August 2, 1976

∞

    keep reading
    keep eating
    keep adding
    and subtracting
    keep confirming
    keep expressing
    keep supposing
    and beginning
    keep it easy—

I never stopped
        trying
        trading
        those integrals

but that's not doing it
you *have to know ahead of time*

shit
I could always predict
but couldn't *make* anything on it!

lacked—still do—more so—
a certain kind of "wit" I so admire
and covet and am entertained by—

the difference between Gene Kelly
and Fred Astaire—

Tom Raworth and Edmund White—

I appreciate and hear them all
the "decongealment" of the
imaginative
function

the ideology of *mass*
they call it "spreading it thin"
two "it" 's contradicting *the* mass
in our home the communion of
"art" in "the masses" of my father
(now dead) saying "work, work, work"
in my head and the rest in *theirs*
the Clint Eastwoods of

                "competence"

imagine the chance again—
nice summer day—1958
at the kitchen sink
getting a drink of water—
sun pouring in through the windows—
two views and the air through
the open "sashes" and the sound
of the traffic—occasional and
distant till a horn honks in
front and you know *it's for you*—
something to do!
(here too—August 1976 New York City—
  the sky is an historical blue
  through the windows and the air
  through the open "casements"—)
shit—*that chance*—"gone"—
and the wit to grasp it with it—

                    October 24, 1951

    ... Oh my goodness, I almost
forgot to tell you. Michael got a
regular report card for the first time

and his average was 97.2. We were
all very excited about it. His marks
were Religion 95, Arith. 96, English 97,
History 98, Reading 99, Geog. 100, Spelling
96, Penmanship (like all the rest of you
kids), 85.
... Michael has a teacher this year (it is
her first year teaching) and she told
Joan that he is a brilliant child (?).
We shall see by the end of the year if
she knows what she is talking about.
I doubt it.

∞

(Miles say six years old and my
love for him a need as well no
"literary" image could unique
just plain vocabulary of respect
always first for the context

∞

I DON'T BELIEVE I CAN'T DO IT

Keep doing it—
keeps us (us) alive—

does that mean
if we don't do it—
fail to do it—
we stop living?—
WE DIE!?

(*they* don't die—not doing it—shit)

anyway—
don't we die doing it too?—
isn't *dying doing* it?—
don't say resist doing it—
don't say Buddhist—

say "it was great fun"—
say what—

        last different ways
        knots are also nipples
        into a shapely, single
        walk—core & all—

yet   moment
while   time
according to   money men
lickety-split   soul searching began in
representing   which
disregard   power people

    and his in this reminder
    the paired oval-shaped portraits of
    The Sacred Heart of Jesus and
    Our Lady of Sorrows—smiling
    down on me—my mother—
    chin resting on temple of folded hands—
    within which memory voids—

the lower-class romanticism of
success determined to be the
answer to love—that question
in taffeta—in violin phone call
tight jean Hollywood sound burst still—

    holding breath—realizing transition
    transitional meditation—
    goddamn it feels good to see
    what it'll do this time—

THE RAIN TRILOGY

1. & Love

this gift
so *right*
afraid to
write—but
today's review
misguided
incorrect—but
"lively" talking
to on-the-phone
from Union Station
half hard just hearing
her voice (saying
"darling"—like
movies last night

glad to "have" not wanting
to take all the chances any more—but
obviously

first work
the new

sort of
a now

make some
do

∞

Alex Katz
wants me
to pose
in my clothes
(I guess)

Nat King Cole
buying Nat
King Cole "I'm

so" fucking
sentimental!

"...someday soon
I'll find you—
somewhere along
the way..."
(Lao Tzu influence!

∞

on an impulse
bought 4 Frank Sinatra
from late 1950s early '60s
& collected piano music of
Charles Ives

another brilliant impulse

what we all share!

∞

7—my son—with me
missing his mother & sister

his sister with his mother
missing him & me—

me missing his sister, having
missed him before he was
with me—everyone sad—

∞

9 years old—my daughter
I wanted to take her with us
I am conciliatory or resigned

∞

rest

∞

working in the kitchen
playing with his "friend"
"sort of" reading in the
bedroom incredible ability
to convey the poignant &
"A Letter to Franz Wright"

"Love"—15-degree weather—city
life last night *Pal Joey* &
Cover Girl & all the illusions—
allusions I *can* go on going on

but how slight & generalized
(*romantic!*) nowhere the precision
inclusiveness of Ponge with "Pebbles"
My new work needs work

So what so glad he is
with me

∞

"boom"   my son
                asleep
crouched at the end
of a narrow bed
"the way he likes it"
& me
          working hard at

"the job"—

like "dues"—
   endless & pointless

call from *her*—
   job no longer "pointless"
   now necessary to make
   money to live "the life"
   (dinner, dance, date,
   "darling"...)—

                ∞

only
when I said I was still
        "married"
she said "go to hell"
meaning—as she
explained later—I was
playing it "safe"—

which is true—
but
I'm "surviving" too—
she still scares me
and says I still scare her
and I do—

                ∞

          like a plug into the
          "intimacy" of teenage

steadies I always missed,
getting "sex" instead,
and mistaking the two—

I'm "crazy about her"—

back to—
            I'm crazy—
"falling in love" like
writing a "poem"—
something I do—

∞

"something I do"—OK—

there's always a
confusion of sighs
and inspiration in
between—but—

"this is different"

∞

to quit my job, become
an actor ("There's too

    —"phew!"—

—"my drummer" 15 years ago!—
called to tell me he loves
me "you goddamn son of
a bitch you know I love you"

            "I love
your lyin' son-of-a-bitching
ass Michael, now
you know I do"

"I swear to god if I were
there I'd suck your dick—
that's the truth of how
much I love you—you
asshole"—

∞

scared & crazy

∞

I'm afraid of the lure
of bars and dancing and
glamour, art world stark
and anguished or just
no kids and their need for
stability and some com-
placency—

stop everything here—

much *love* and *rightness*

it's totally insane and
teenage and exhausting—

I have lived for and
taken so many chances
on people for—and never
thought I'd really

∞

                    shit—
I *need* her
and a month ago
I didn't even *know* her—

but
at least I'm finally
taking care of *that*—

∞

now "we'll see"—but
it looks like we're
gonna do our best
                —spend her nights
            with me—her days
            or whatever being free
            to compose or work or
            —I want her near me
            all the time—but I

do my own work—
and work out a way
to live by working

now—to work—for
what?—money to do
it all—and what will
this job matter if I
never or ever get "the
writing" done—not
even "fun"—just dumb—

∞

a double LP of
Lester Young sets—
so nice I listen to each
twice—and the
Philip Glass album
—*North Star*—
                dug by
me & somewhat by "she"

I just flash all day
on her smile and touch
and all the good things
I love so much—

everything—oh oh oh—

"what it's all about"
—for *me*—

∞

she brought it up
& I suggested she
just tell me from
now on when she
had ex-lovers to see
etc.—that she
"had work to do"
that night but
she said: "No—
I'm as compulsively
honest as you
are"—!—(which
of course made me
secretly *happy*—but

∞

meanwhile Miles
cried after *West
Side Story* (on TV)
"not because I'm
sad—but because
it was *so good*"
said it was his
favorite movie—even
better than *Star
Wars*
            —later
said he'd wear his

levis, a plain tee
shirt ("no writing
on it") and his
reversible jacket
with the beige side
out—as an extension
of *West Side Story* style—
7 years old!—a "genius"

∞

defending our plan
to move in together

against questions
about how she will

what about my
writing?)—(her

I said maybe we've
discovered the next
kind of coupling emotion
beyond the "love" we've
inherited from the
renaissance?—)—now
just want to find a
place (loft probably)
and get the divorce
and do the writing
and composing and
the jobs to pay the
bills—and be happy

∞

& scary
& her showing up
looking hurt

∞

&
(part two)

   I don't
want—or like being
the cause of

 "insecure" all

total devotion to her

together forever

∞

still not only "good"
but getting *better!*

made love 4 times after
waking up—3 times before
going to sleep!—and
could've kept going

∞

played for me at last

"easy listening" she said

I wanted to cry and
laugh and *everything*

so sophisticated but
pure—she's gonna
have a hard time

∞

I read my *Oomaloom*

got as "insecure"
self-conscious
embarrassed and
withdrawn
                —the
"truth" of those

my attempts to capture
the various poses
and articulations

sexual roles I had
"tried out" or been

                ∞

rain rain lays me
                back
makes me feel the
                magic
in the atmosphere
                again

the "life force-flow"
is back in the right
space here in my
personal specialty—
I'm making it on
less attention these
days and satisfying
the peace needs—

                ∞

the "big book"
still inside my

"novel" "epic"
"poem" "new form"
"what?" too much
ask me by me
who else

god what a beautiful
this that avoided it

                the

the sunsets from
the Chrysler Building & beyond

    & *love*

2. *May 25, 1978*

36 today. Doesn't seem as significant as turning 35 last year. But still causing all kinds of memories, flashes of the way I thought it might be, is, has been, might become, etc. Had a restless night because of this, brain too busy with 36 years of fast changes in the most fulfilling experiences my intelligence can make snap decisions for with survival still a prerequisite, attempting to outwit fate, etc.

Got up at my usual workday 7 A.M. or so, the "or so" the moments spent copping a few more zz's, enjoying the warmth and delicate strength of Rain's body against mine, whispering whatever extensions on last night's love words this all generates, trying to communicate with my skin and lips and heart as much of my love and lust for her as I can without getting too excited since there's not enough time to make love and besides Miles might stumble in and besides according to the docs I'm supposed to take it easy on my prostate and pecker and the rest of the plumbing that counts. Thinking about that as I rise—about the irony of having love and sex as the obsessions of my 36 years, even more than most, and only discovering how to truly enjoy as well as get it in the past several years only to end up with physical ailments usually reserved for men twice my age if at all, well it's not that bad, I can still do almost everything, I just can't do it as many times a day as

I used to and would like to or for as long as I used to and like to and sometimes even then it hurts. I go in and help Miles decide on what he will wear to third grade today considering the weather report which I got over the phone while still in bed.

While Miles dresses I go out to the hall to the funky bathroom in which the plaster is falling from the ceiling, giant ugly moldy holes from 100 years of use without repairs. I sit on the broken wooden toilet seat, which actually always feels warm and much more comfortable than all the modern plastic and other synthetic ones. I always sit when at home, ever since living in a collective with nine lesbian feminists and me the only male. At one of the collective meetings, at which we usually discussed me and my habits, since I was the only male and for reasons too complex to go into here had willingly subjected myself to this experiment and experience to find out what I could about the parts of me I might not otherwise have discovered or come to know so well and also to find out about the way others could be that I had never seen up close before and also to see if I could become a better human, kinder and more considerate of others who might not be like me, and more. At any rate one of the issues that came up early was my leaving the toilet seat up after pissing, especially late at night, and one of them getting up and going out half asleep to sit down and discover they were on the hard, cold, thinner rim of the toilet itself, maybe even fearing for their safety as they realized they were descending lower than they had expected and coming awake abruptly only to realize it was just my fault again. Others also complained of the macho implications of the loud noise pissing standing up always caused, especially considering the bathroom I usually used was right off the kitchen, and often we didn't close the door since we were also freedom-loving bohemian-hippie types at the time too. Actually most of these women were nothing of the sort but had become that under the influence of my wife and me. Sort of a meeting of the intransigent feminist dyke psyche with the open to experience bohemian (what a terrible word, but what would fit better that isn't already out of fashion— we were called "beatniks" and "hippies" and "hipsters" and "fringies" and several other terms more or less fashionable at different times but of course we never called ourselves any of this shit, in fact what we called ourselves was usually inaccurate, like my wife calling herself "lesbian" when she was still apt to get angry at me for not making love to her enough, or me calling myself a "faggot" when I was still overwhelmingly hungry for the bodies of women I passed on the street or saw in the movies or glanced at in advertisements in magazines or whatever—although we had good reasons, namely that by publicly identifying with an oppressed group that we were part of sometimes, because we also did make love to those of our own sex and dug it, we were making a political statement of solidarity and refusing to enjoy the benefits we might have accrued by letting ourselves be identified with any groups easier for society to accept like say "bisexuals," the horrible term for people who certainly must be aware as I was that there is nothing "bi" anything about sex with different sexes, there are so many kinds of people, much more than two, or like say straight hippies or whatever which were at the time—early '70s—becoming more and more acceptable or dismissable) ... anyway, it made a certain kind of sense to me at the time to respect their wishes and try pissing while sitting and what I discovered among other things, like identifying even further with women, was that it was a lot more convenient, neater, peaceful, and relaxing to sit down while pissing and so I continue to do it to this day. It also makes it easy to read/ or take a shit if that happens to come up while you're at it.

So this morning I took a copy of *Mag City* #4, a magazine put out by some of the younger poets I've run into in the past few years, mostly around St. Mark's, which one of them gave me last night when we went to a benefit at St. Mark's to raise money for the "Poetry Project" which is what stimulates or at least originally generated much of the activity that still attracts young poets and sometimes others of us to that part of town (of course many of them say they live there 'cause it's cheap, but there's tons of cheap neighborhoods in the city and a lot of them more interesting and rewarding than that part of the lower east side that the church is near). I sit down, a bit hesitant because it's so cold and damp in the bathroom after a night of rain and temperatures in the 50s, but the wooden seat warms up quickly and I get into the magazine, reading through the first several pages, wondering why there is always mention of someone I know but never of me when I've been around publishing and influencing in the small press poetry scene for many years—longer than almost any of the poets associated with St. Mark's, in fact longer than any of the "New York" poets except the originals who began in the late '40s and early '50s. I began in 1960, writing out of my experiences on the lower east side, in fact, among other things, being rejected for writing

108

about growing up in the '50s with rock'n'roll, and for my pre-hippie dope visions and proto-political philosophy of creative humanism and all that. This kind of thinking can only lead to disappointing conclusions of course, like that these kids just don't like me that much, or probably more accurately, don't like my work or think it that important, despite the fact that many of them have obviously been influenced directly or indirectly by the chances I've taken over the years. The St. Mark's crew of my generation having taken very few chances, and those always with the support of a group that no matter how diversified and full of its own infighting and competitiveness nonetheless knows how to close ranks and defend its own whenever an "outsider" raises any objections or attempts to get some attention or equal recognition from some of the same constituency. *Constituency* is a better word for it than *audience* too because that's pretty much the way that scene treats its audience, like they're voters to be cajoled or bullied bribed or tricked or swayed or whatever into supporting the St. Mark's ticket. See where this kind of thinking leads? Shit, it's like the benefit last night, pretty disappointing.

In fact I rarely go to St. Mark's to a reading or meeting, or a party that the central St. Mark's group attends or one of them throws that I don't come away somehow anxious or sad or disappointed or depressed or angry. Very rarely do I come away feeling terrific and happy and glad to be alive and a poet and a human and all the ways I have felt, and others have told me they have felt, when they came away from readings or parties or whatever that I had anything to do with setting up or carrying out over the years, and likewise for most of my friends who are outside or only on the edges of that scene. So I'm already feeling a bit glum and the day has hardly begun and it's my birthday too when I turn to a piece by Bernadette Mayer that is a journal entry, something like this, but of course my journal entries are usually nothing like this, so I am in debt to Bernadette for getting me into this mode, at any rate, she mentions my name and it startles me. Then I see what she is doing. I think. I'm only part of the mail, and it's only a review I did of some of her books that came out a few years ago. The review was in *The Washington Post*, the editor of which I convinced to let me do reviews of small press books because I wanted to share my own enthusiasms and also because I wanted to help create a wider audience for those I thought should have that. The usual altruistic stuff that misleads me and perhaps you, 'cause I am writing this to be read, just as Bernadette seems to write her journal entries, and probably most of us poets do, to be read by others, not only because it helps get us through the day and our lives as poets and writers who have few reasons besides our own compulsions to continue doing something so few are into and most of them are other writers and poets who want our attention too. For me books have always been a way of saving my life, keeping me from total self-destruction. I read something and it reminds me of all the other stuff, and all the stuff in me that I could only see as part of my peculiar struggle or glee, all that. At any rate I always loved reading and still do, but in recent years I have come away from reading stuff out of St. Mark's with more and more bad feelings. For whatever reasons that are uniquely mine and the other reasons that obviously a wider audience shares since there exists such animosity to that scene.

Something I tried to warn Padgett about after he became the director of the place, only to have my words misinterpreted as some "personal thing between" me and Anne Waldman when in fact the only personal thing between Anne and me is an occasional conversation at some social event. All this shit is going around in my brain as I read through Bernadette's piece making a connection between her mentioning receiving the review by me and then a series of things that bug her including people always saying or writing the same thing about her work as though only one person read it and then everyone else copied from that. Does she mean my review? Was she disappointed that I praised her and recommended her work and pointed out how important she was as an innovator and influence? I told her some of these things the first time I met her. And once I brought some other writers who write something like her to hear her read in Philadelphia, when me and the writers lived in DC (it was Tina Darragh and Lynne Dreyer) and Bernadette seemed to think that these were followers of hers as though there weren't people out there writing like her before her and along with her who didn't know of her work (even though she, like most of the other members of my generation of St. Mark's associated poets seem to be very limited in their knowledge of the work of contemporaries outside that scene, in fact it is another reason paying attention to that scene always leaves some of us feeling badly about poets and especially St. Mark's because even though most of us are poor, hassling with the shit of trying to be a poet and survive, avoiding all the copouts that lead to the

110

work becoming less important, etc., etc. we seem to manage, at least me and most of the poets I know do, to check out the work of others in magazines and books that come along or that we buy or browse through in the stores or pass on to each other).

"Oh well," I think as I go back into the loft to make breakfast for Miles and me, first helping him find a longsleeve shirt with no buttons and not turtleneck which he claims there are none of on the bookcase shelf we use to store his clothes but of course I find one instantly and he says something like "How come I didn't see that? Where *was* it?!" and so on, feigning the usual kid astonishment when you take care of business for them because to some extent they're still used to that. Or maybe it's just him that's used to it because sometimes I spoil him a little as a result of our having lived the bachelor life alone together and his having to put up with my steady stream of lovers and even when I was monogamous there were changes in who I was monogamous with that left him a little dazed sometimes as well as me. But now we've been together with Rain for one year, well I met her a year ago on the night of my annual birthday party so we've really only all been living together since September, which makes it 8 months, though from the moment we met we never went to bed with anyone else again and in my mind that's like living together, in fact even more than living together that's the romantic real love stuff that makes life worth all the bumping around and frustration that even Miles at 8 years old has to face. Although he seems less obsessed with some of that stuff than I was at his age, having very early gotten into the search for true love. Anyway, I run through breakfast, make his lunch for him, continually coaxing him to move along so he won't be late, then take a shower yelling to Rain to answer the phone because Miles is out in the bathroom (the shower's in the tub which is in the kitchen) and I'm in the shower. She says OK and the ringing stops, she's still in bed but I know the phone call unless it's a wrong number will wake her up so that she'll decide to get up and I won't get to give her one more kiss in bed which is always a treat before I leave for work, though some mornings she does get up and help with breakfast and make Miles' lunch and mine and that's great too because then we get to touch and brush against each other a few times while passing in and out of the kitchen and bedroom (which is also a workroom for both of us, my desk and typewriter and books and files and her piano).

In the shower I'm half happy to be alive and awake and still determined and curious after 36 years, and half disturbed by my own mind's crazy vulnerability to that St. Mark's syndrome. Why should I give a fuck? Because I am one of those who noticed the work of these jokers and liked a lot of it and saw things I thought we had in common and so reviewed it favorably using my then pretty hotstuff reputation in the small press world to try and turn folks on to the work of young poets who were at that time (late '60s) pretty unknown outside their own scene, and because in doing so I lost my position as small press hotshot poet, the daring that made me famous (so to speak) and popular (it seemed so odd at the time but there were tons of strangers in almost every place I ever lived, and I tend to move more often than there are years in my life, who knew me and somehow appreciated me and let me know it which always confused and slightly embarrassed me and was one of the reasons I returned to New York for the anonymity possible here) suddenly made me one of those and I bore the brunt of much of the small press scene's bad feelings for this group I was only beginning to appreciate. But I stuck by my guns and all that, hoped I wasn't being unkind to any former fans and friends, but like when admitting to having sex with some men and being a sissy sometimes when it comes to much macho bullshit and all that, I lost part of my audience and some of those who had "discovered" me at one time or another as they saw me slip into the world of the "New York School" scene, which was all part of the same thing in their minds as the St. Mark's scene (as it is in some of the minds of some of the St. Mark's scene). What the fuck, I was only doing what I have always made one of the major goals of my writing and life and all that: trying to be as honest and as clear about it as might be possible for me. And then I started meeting some of these poets I was now championing (like the calling myself a "faggot" number, I was defending them a little too strenuously only because they were being attacked everywhere I went and me with them so strenuously, when in fact much of the writing I found incredibly uneven, and more so as the years passed and there seemed to develop a kind of self-parody among those who had seemed to have the most promise and an imitative homage to that self-parody by those who had never shown much promise at all but had gotten equal attention just for being successful at becoming an integral part of that scene—or so it appeared from the outside, which despite the shit I was getting from those who thought I was in, was where I was and remain).

They turned out to be warm and funny and pretty regular folks when I lived out of town (and that made it easier to dismiss the fact that they had rejected my poems for their magazines over the years and put me off in other ways that seemed kind of arbitrary and even condescending at times although it never seemed to matter that much at the time to me since I was publishing all over the place almost all the time and figured they just couldn't hear the work because I came from such a different place than them despite what I thought we had in common in terms of technical risk taking and being outside the academic tradition and loving New York and believing in the future and so on) and came in for a visit or they came to do a reading I had set up or gone to hear. Then I moved here and discovered that I really was an outsider. I didn't expect much except to be treated the same way here as I was when I ran into them elsewhere. But there seemed to be some invisible system of ranking always at work which determined their behavior toward me in any given situation and which also began more and more to appear calculated and deliberately mean. I was so surprised I just didn't believe it. I kept going to the readings at the Church (as those who frequent the place begin to call it, just as when I was a kid growing up in New Jersey we used to refer to New York as "the city" whenever we were talking about going there or something that was happening there and to Newark as "downtown") and kept socializing with the folks there whenever I was invited to and soon I saw that they caused as much anxiety and competitiveness and hurt feelings among themselves as they did for others and that began to make me wonder what the value of their scene was.

But, still, in New York at any rate, the reading series at St. Mark's is one of the most interesting, one of the easiest to get to if you live downtown, and I did happen to *know* a lot of the people over there and I'm a poet too and I know some of them knew some of my work since they had seen it when it was submitted to their magazines and they rejected it and/or they must have seen it when we appeared in the same magazines together over the years and/or some of them had mentioned some of my work to me at different times, though usually not in any overwhelmingly flattering way, more like "I saw that poem of yours in —— mag, pretty strange." Once, Lewis Warsh complimented me on my poem "My Life" which had appeared in *ZZZ*, and several younger poets had complimented me for the same poem. Of course, I realized as I

113

was drying off and in between continuing to coax Miles to go catch the bus for school while he continued blowing bubbles (we had both eaten our breakfast and taken our vitamins before I got into the shower) that as usual whenever I thought about St. Mark's I was blowing everything out of proportion because in fact many of the poets associated with that place had admired my work over the years and told me so many times, or responded to specific work. But then, how come none of them ever came to my readings I thought as I was getting dressed and Rain was already out of bed and beginning to do some photography work that she does at home for a living to support her life as a composer who has to face some of the same shit any creative person does in trying to make a living and have her work heard and so on but she refuses to fall into the same self-defeating hang-ups as some of us poets get into with "scenes" and "audiences" and ego. One of the many reasons I admire her as well as love her. And it reminds me that there's no sense in this line of thought but I explain to her anyway what's on my mind and she asks me once again why I even care about people who seem to cause so much bad feelings. Well, they cause good feelings sometime too, right? Or at least some of their work does, or has. O well, I have to get to work.

Miles finally leaves, and I'm worried because it's so late that he might really miss the bus, though he says he's missed it already and just walked to school. He's getting really independent at last which relieves me and scares me at the same time. In fact, for a while he was sneaking on the subway and taking that to school and back until I found out and told him not to. He's pretty good still about listening to my advice, I hope that lasts until he's old enough to take care of himself all the way. But thinking about Miles just reminds me of all the excuses I've heard over the years from St. Mark's poets with kids about how they couldn't make a reading of mine or some other thing I was interested in, when of course, I have kids, and at one time it was just me and him, and I have been poor most of my adult life (and despite my recent and naturally short-lived "good job" through which many of the younger St. Mark's scene poets have been able to make money, as I am in charge of handing out some pretty lucrative freelance writing assignments and always want to help out poor poets since I'm one too because even with this job I have so many debts from before, I got no extra coin anyway and no extra time either like they do, someone recently pointed out to me that most of the poets who

114

I've helped out, and whose writing I've had to make excuses for or rewrite or apologize for because they are usually not up to this particular kind of hack writing, have begun to treat me like some booshwa uptown dude relating to me only as a source of extra income and never relating to me as a poet but instead always casting themselves in that role of poor struggling artist when in fact most of them have parents to hit up if they have to and as much education as me—and I got it much later going back to school in my late 20s on the GI Bill—and are in better physical shape and have no kids and have a scene and group to support their egos when for me at their age I was constantly getting kicked out of groups and scenes for saying what was on my mind or for being too street-oriented in some of the ways I express myself and my energy and ambition and joy and frustration and all) anyway it struck me that being poor and/or having kids is no excuse for others when it hasn't been for me. So the only other reason they skip my readings or the readings of my friends is that they don't like the work or think we as poets aren't important enough to follow even if they don't like the work (because they are always at readings of St. Mark's scene originals even when they admit privately they don't think much of the stuff).

Rain once again tells me to just ignore those people and that scene and swears she isn't going to St. Mark's unless it's something she knows she likes since so often it has been disappointing like the benefit the night before, and besides there's so much else to check out and do it's too much of a waste of time. I agree, though I know I'm still stuck in this train of thought, a phrase that Bernadette also used when writing the entry that sparked all this, so maybe now I understand how she could write something that might be misinterpreted as I suppose this will be when it appears as just more sour grapes as did some of her piece to me. So after some private stuff between Rain and me that leaves us as much or more in love than ever and wishing I could stay home and share more of the day with her I go to work in my suit and tie mindful of the promise I made myself when I graduated from grammar school that I would never wear a tie again because I was going to public school after that and planned a life free of the constraints of ties and shit even then. But the bishop persuaded my father to send me to another Catholic school by promising to pay the bills for it, a prep school in Newark, a day school full of scholarship students and middle-class fuck-offs whose parents didn't have the money to send them somewhere more classy or thought it would straighten them out to go to St. Benedict's which in the '50s when I went there was in the middle of a tough black neighborhood later trivialized with the media term *ghetto* after the riots of the '60s originated there. Back then it was just more of an ongoing education in black culture I had already immersed myself in and got into even further as it became clear where the lack of constraints were in 1950's Newark and the rest of New Jersey. At any rate, here I am again in a tie, but I've already promised myself a birthday present of quitting this gig by the end of summer. So I can take it till then, and besides I like paying the bills and being able to be free of the nagging that has accompanied poverty with most of my mates and lovers and kids and friends.

On the subway the pretty women on their way to work make the morning seem nicer than the drizzly weather has. At least it isn't freezing as it has been all winter. I bought a copy of the *Daily News* and *The Village Voice* on the way to the subway so now I open them and check them out. *The Voice* is not a favorite but since they hired me to write about small press books and then fired me after I had satisfied them with one big article more or less in their style and then tried to bring it around more to my style and cover less trendy and gossipy stuff and what I think is more significant and interesting in terms of contemporary writing. Once again the old altruistic championing of the difficult or contrary writing of the small press scene has taken bread from my mouth so to speak, as Andrei Codrescu once claimed I had done by reviewing a book of his for the *Washington Post* in which I made great claims for him as a poet and half-praised the book (*The Life and Times of an Involuntary Genius*) and then expressed disappointment in his not telling us more about what it was really like to grow up in a Communist country and be my age and be fairly hip and then come to the USA and discover a community of hip poets who embraced you. And that takes me back to the St. Mark's crowd because that was the crowd he became a part of for a while upon his arrival from his travels through Europe after escaping from Romania which doesn't seem all that bad a place the way he describes it since the biggest hassle he mentions is with the draft, not unknown to my generation in the USA and some Communist Party official was the key to helping him escape, which escape took place by getting on a nice flight out of the

116

country like anyone leaving the States who this government isn't trying to stop.

Shit. I'm right back where I started from, thinking how some St. Mark's folks told me that Codrescu couldn't really write the truth about his Romanian background because it was all made up anyway, they weren't sure where he was from and that reminded me of talking to another poet from that scene the other night at a party at which many from that scene were milling about making each other and me self-conscious in ways that are a drag, especially at a party, though I was so high it was more a part of my stoned theater than any kind of effective reality, at any rate she uttered surprise to discover I'd moved twice since the last place she visited me at only a year ago, and I admitted I was tired of moving so much and wished I could stay someplace for a while but something always seemed to come up, which is why I had moved 26 times since leaving home 18 years ago, at which she showed even more amazement saying something like "Gee, I never realized that stuff in your poetry was actually true."

And then I remembered how when I first met her she was very cautious about becoming my friend, though I liked her and her work and once again used whatever influence and cachet I might have to get her readings and attention outside that scene, even so she continued to be defensive and overly cautious with me and let other people know she thought my work was not so hot, though finally she admitted I seemed nice enough. It turned out that Larry Fagin, who I have only spoken to about three times in my life more than a nod or hello, and then he did all the talking, had told her and others how I was this totally ambitious "careerist" whose poetry wasn't worth anything but who was useful as a reviewer! Goddamn! My paranoia around those nerds is actually justified! But so what? I don't think much of Fagin's poetry either, and it is true that I am ambitious, though I can't imagine a poet or writer who wouldn't want to see his or her work in print and available to the largest audience possible and especially to those people who seem to share some of the same ideas and taste and so on.

Well, I get off the subway and walk the three blocks to the job thinking about how that scene has generated some great work that might have been written otherwise and might not have, but that most of this terrific stuff was written by the poets that scene seems to treat as the least important among them—like say Ted

Greenwald or Harris Schiff or—but no that isn't true, Berrigan and Notley and others who are treated very well, or at least with the respect their work seems to deserve a lot of the time...o, it don't make sense and isn't supposed to. It's just a scene, and because it happened to be in New York and happened to take a lot of its cues from people good at manipulating the media and getting attention for lifestyle and personality as much as for the actual work—like Ginsberg—a lot of them got more attention than perhaps their work deserved or than other people as good or better ever got in their more obscure scenes around the country and even in New York in their isolation. Then Ginsberg coming to mind sets the stage for the whole thing, after meeting him I'd guess about 200 times or so since the late '50s, he has never said hello to me or spoken to me on his own except once, several years ago, after a review of mine appeared in the *Washington Post* again (Bill McPherson being the only editor I've encountered so far adventurous enough to use non-academic writers to do reviews and to cover what they think is important and not only what the *Times* and "the publishing industry" thinks is). I had reviewed the first three books in the Full Court list, and in the process said some nice things about Ginsberg even though it was a book of his I would not keep around, still he's done important things. It was Edwin Denby's and Joe Brainard's books I was really praising, at any rate I was at a Gotham Book Mart book party shortly after it appeared and Ginsberg approached me because I was talking to some pretty young boy who was with him at the time though I hadn't known that when I started talking to him, and as he cut in on our conversation he acknowledged me by mentioning the *Post* review and it occurred to me that all the times we'd run into each other over the years he must have known who I was and just never let that come out till I did this article about him, contributing to the newsworthiness of his name by keeping it in the news. Since then I've seen him another hundred times or whatever and once again he totally ignores me even if I'm talking to someone he comes up to talk to. What ego us poets have, maybe because the rewards are so few and the audiences are so limited and made up mostly of us and other poets anyway. But whatever it is by the time I get to work I'm already exhausted mentally from all these down thoughts so I close the door to my office and sit down at this great IBM typewriter which I will miss and spend the morning typing out this to get it over once and for all my farewell to St.

Mark's and the confusion and frustration and hurt it has caused me and so many others I know, despite the many fine people who are still around that scene and have always been and probably will be long after they forget that I ever passed through it.

3. *1979, etc.*

—then at CBGB we found an enormous, hot, stuffy, impolite, wired crowd—the band played too long & then Ginsberg read too long so that by the time John Cale & friends (Ivan Kral, et al.) got up to jam—it was already past 1 A.M. & I was supposed to go on at midnight—after John Cale it was past 2 and many folks left—but there was still a full house when Ted B. introduced me saying something like "Michael Lally is the most notorious sexual outlaw in the country, he comes to us from the Air Force, a few juvenile penitentiaries, a few Ph.Ds and" something something etc.—

∞

then I got up to very sparse applause, obviously most of the people didn't know who I was or care—but Ginsberg, Orlovsky, John Giorno, Waldman (who "made up" with me earlier at the table the poets were sharing) & Berrigan were up front & did—I just introduced the poem saying "I'm going to read a piece I wrote for myself several years ago when I was turning 32—I'd like to dedicate it tonight to Ted Berrigan" then I went right into "My Life" & read it loud & fast—really fast—I could feel a lot of people getting with it & I could hear an occasional heckler (mostly one woman, to whom I slipped out the aside: "It's *my* life baby") or something—at any rate as I got into it I heard myself of 4 or 5 years ago speaking to me now—a more open and in some ways wiser me then—giving me & these punks and punk fans some advice—good advice—and honesty about fear & vulnerability as well as despair & dues & etc.—it felt good—so good that when I finished I didn't care if they liked it or not—I had loved it—& as it turned out, so did a lot of them—the applause was tremendous even with shouts of "More" etc.—& the bartenders sent me a free drink saying they "were really moved" & "what the hell was my *name*?!"—& others came by to ask for names of books & my name & to tell me how they were impressed—and then on our way out several people

reached out to touch me & tell me how much they had dug it (one
guy at the bar, nice looking & straight, non-punk, non-gay looking
told me how "moved" he was by it—& Peter Gordon said I was
real "powerful" up there)—it was a regular triumph—& I felt a little like a "rock star" for the rest of the night which me & Rain
spent getting high(er) & talking (crashed finally near 5 A.M.)—etc.

∞

still getting reaction from the CBGB gig—Tom Carey called—
spoke with Rain since I was out—told her my bit had "raised the
consciousness of the whole benefit" etc.—okay—next?—(I guess
the people who become "stars" would have had agents and publi-
cists and etc. at that thing to show them their stuff—I always
expected) "them" (the people with power etc.) to just *be there*
sometime when I'm doing it & sign me *up!*—

∞

reading *The Saddest Story* about Ford Madox Ford (the bio)—I
can see how I better be careful or my "need to set the record
straight" will leave me much maligned after I'm gone for my "vanity" or "weakness" or etc.—shit maybe he *did* influence Conrad!—
& *me!*—

∞

… another "misunderstanding"—something she feels we've been
having a lot of lately—partly because we're both so frustrated in
our "ambitions"—she wants to be "famous" etc. & "great" (she *is*
"great" but she, like me, wants recognition for it or the chance to
show it or share it or whatever)—I got my main manuscript of
major poems ("My Life," "All of the Above" etc.) back from
Penguin *even though* their readers loved it, their editors loved it,
their publicity people loved it—etc.

∞

… so Rain has been saying things like how she doesn't want to just
give up and live an ordinary life—be a housewife or a photo-
graphic processor or whatever—she said if she couldn't do her
own thing maybe she could become famous as the "mistress" (her

120

term) of famous people—as though our "love" had nothing to do with it or wasn't as important or *more* important than her "fame" etc.—*not good*—

∞

at least I keep getting good feedback from the CBGB benefit— Tim D. ran into Allen Ginsberg in Philly & A.G. told him how great I was & how I was the high spot of the night etc. etc.—

∞

tonight we're supposed to go to a party at Karen's agent's—a big deal—with the important people—& I don't know how we'll go over—we're such semi-bohemians "dressing up" and "going out" etc. is always a little too "challenging"—!—

∞

... I did *not* have a very good time or make a very big hit or find it easy to talk to & be with those "showbiz" folks—they all seemed "on" & working at it in one way or the other—just a case of "getting to know" them I guess—but I really didn't feel any urge to— ... (interrupted by the mice in the ceiling—so loud, screeching & scrambling that Rain came in from the other room to check it out!—"Life!"—when will it be "easy"—again)!—etc.

∞

... me & Ted G, at the Ukrainian bar & Ginsberg comes in with others and spends some time talking—asking about my work etc.—wanting to see my books—offering advice about publishing etc.—nice, maybe it'll come to something, but I couldn't help thinking "*too late!*"

∞

In fact much of what I'm going through lately (... acting in student films, etc.) keeps me feeling not only that I've been here before & should be further along—but that I'm once again "losing my innocence" & feeling the need to rediscover some "dream" some hope some belief that my life & the way I see myself having lived it by standards and goals that I believe are more human and positive than those I've been given or had imposed on me (& the rest of the world) should have more rewards than pretty regular minor aggravations & responsibilities & a lot of hard work to get one-hundredth as much as I desire & feel I deserve etc. etc.

∞

tomorrow I do this new NYU student film—shades of Val Ryker in '66 at Iowa or Gary Williams in '64 in Spokane (when I played "Baby Face Nelson" in his version of *Dillinger*) etc.—I just wanna be the *real thing!*

∞

have so much to do
& I'm not doing
any of it
etc.

∞

(reading Laura Riding
& Gerald Burns)
(talking with Miles—football,
school, food, the past, etc. & reading to him
from William Saroyan story collection)

∞

did a movie this week—NYU student silent flick—(dir: Robert Becker "co-star" Patricia?) before doing it felt depressed—I did these silent student shorts in Spokane & Iowa 14 and 12 years ago!?—I've gotten *nowhere* (as a "movie star")—*but*—then I did it & it felt so good—it didn't matter—just *doing* it was so much fun—being "an actor" or even "a film actor"—sitting around drinking coffee (or hot chocolate) while "the crew" sets up the shots etc. etc.—discussing "the bizniz" with my fellow (*sister!*) actor—etc. and "taking direction" & just fucking *doing it*—now I can't wait to see it—maybe Saturday night I'll go screen the footage—be nice—Patricia was nice too—lot of similar opinions & takes (though not as smart or soft?—no vulnerable—as Rain (& *me*)—but still unlike the actors & actresses we've been meeting so far—

∞

low on money—depending on Rain for too much—she said she wanted it this way (only for this winter then I've got to make it or go back to ugh jobs)—*but I should know better*—no $—no good vibes—etc.

∞

I don't know how extraordinary I am (might be/have been)—my friends—most—over the years—have always led me to believe I was/am—but in the past it was because of the way I saw/see the world and react to it and act in it—whereas now it is often because of what I say & share about myself—& sometimes *that* seems less than extraordinary and just bragging—etc.

∞

meanwhile I have schemes to take out ads in the *Soho News* & *The Village Voice* etc.—to advertise my books & readings—saying things like "before Punk—before Patti Smith—before Bruce Springsteen (still upset over Susan Wechsler's friend saying she couldn't finish *The South Orange Sonnets* because it "sounded too much like Bruce"!)—*there was LALLY!* etc.

∞

> Dear Mike
> I am with
> John riding
> our bikes
> outside
>
> XXXXX
> XXXXX
> OOOOO

my son—   & me—
             our *love*—
         what I had long wanted—
more than etc.

∞

                    raining

                    I love it

                dark days in the city

                    somehow
                    so many in the '50s
                        early '60s—when I was
                    here—considering it *home*
                    no matter where I was
                    "stationed" or coming from—

                alone on the wet streets
                        cold, but not freezing—
                        reading the
                                atmosphere
                        the sound of the car tires
                        on the slick dark
                        the ways the water
                                falling makes *everyone*
                                eccentric
                                        and alone—

                        I always loved rainy days like today
so much more than etc.

                            ∞

totally exhausted—from Jane's party (for her novel *Some Do*)—at
Tim's (& Bobby Thompson's)—her agent (Jane Rotrosen) told
Michael Dennis (?) (editor at St. Martin's & novelist) that I was
an overwhelmingly talented writer—"the best writer of eroticism"
she'd read—unfortunately the book she was referring to (in MS
form) (*A Dislocation*) she also thinks is "unpublishable" (at least
"commercially")—et*fucking*cetera …

                            ∞

earlier in the day I visited Ginsberg with some of my books for his
interest & to help me get published as he said he would—had a

124

little breakfast with him & he was nice—said something about have I read "the other working man poet"!? etc.—& talked a lot about Cassady as though there is a connection—which I think there is—I guess—& I'm avoiding it 'cause it isn't about the best stuff necessarily—

∞

then took on a freelance editing writing job for St. Mark's!—bad pay but I'm desperate again! so fucking etc.

∞

now my other student director—Sue Green—is bugging me for too much of my time for a classroom exercise! but I committed myself to it—shit—too much to do & not enough will make me money or any happier—etc.

∞

running myself "ragged"
(as me mother—"god rest her soul"—
used to say)—for what?—
nothing—student flicks &
favors & mirages & etc.—
what about
me!?

∞

...meanwhile Rain & Miles & I had Thanksgiving dinner at the Spring Street Bar—a miserable rainy day—but I took Miles & one of his friends (Caleb) to the parade—saw Bucky Dent on a float & the Smothers Brothers & Diana Ross & etc. etc.—they dug it—we could've spent T-day with relatives or friends but I figured Rain could use the time to get ready for her "concert" at *Ear Inn* this Sunday

∞

Miles is 9 today! no etc.

∞

Rain's "concert" at *Ear Inn* yesterday OK—piano *terrible*—nice but
small crowd—good folks though—Karen Allen showed up—& Joe
Brainard—& Ted G. & Joan S. & Doug still in town from DC (his
reading the day before very nice)—etc.

∞

—but bad news last night from the lady upstairs (Alice) on the
new landlord—he came by to tell her he plans to renovate this
Spring & will want us out then so he can do it—she explained all
our leases go for at least 2 more years but he said they weren't
really legal anyway—so he intends, coldly, to put us out—we'll
lose the $5,000 fixture fee we paid the lady who lived here—plus
the $2,000 or so we put into the place (Rain's darkroom, plumb-
ing, etc.)—plus two years of relatively cheap rent plus this beautiful location (which has also been so *good* for Miles)—so I'm pretty
upset—Rain too—fantasizing all kinds of schemes to get the fucking landlord—they are such *scum*—coldly deciding to disrupt and
fuck up & perhaps destroy people's lives & homes so they can
make a buck—I wish there was a revolutionary group that dealt
with landlords—

∞

Shelly Messing called to tell me that she took *Just Let Me Do It* to
Greece and read it on the beach in Crete (?) exclaiming to all who
would listen that it's the best book of poetry she's read "in
years"!—etc.—making me feel pretty good—real good in fact—
and only wishing the critics & powerful were as hip & generous
though Jane DeLynn's review of *Catch My Breath* in the new
(Dec.) St. Mark's *Poetry Project Newsletter* also came out today & is
the best I've ever had—concentrating on my *choices* & why she
thinks it should be obvious to intelligent readers why I make them
etc. etc.—great statements about my work including a comparison
of *The S. O. Sonnets* to Mick Jagger's "Satisfaction"—*all right!*—

∞

trying to do too much
& getting nothing done
—novel for Jane's agent
—lyrics to Tom Moshier's tunes

126

—guide for Franklin Library
(& I'm broke now, living
off Rain's meager earnings)
(not true—she has savings
she put away while she lived off me)
—plays
—poems
—proposals
—flyers for readings
—etc.—etc.—etc.—etc.

and *acting*
(class, auditions, etc.)
!?!?!?!

∞

had lunch with Bambi—she looks older—a touch heavier—but still beautiful—said I looked younger than when she met me (18 years ago!)—nice talk—no passion or smoldering etc.—just keeping in touch & all—

∞

Lee & Boo here with Cait... Cait really looking great—taller & thinner & more beautiful (pretty? "attractive"?—something!)—almost 11—see some of me in her finally—her & Miles good to each other—Lee all right—Boo OK too—though I wouldn't want them around for long, etc.
good visit with Cait—wish she could live with me—

∞

saw Sue Green's "rushes" today—I didn't *look* bad—acted pretty nicely for the most part—didn't pull off the ending at all the way she wanted it—
she insulted me afterwards, talking about how it wasn't enough to just put my pretty face in front of the camera—etc.—
                              "oh well"

∞

feel like I'm coming apart—trying to do too much—doing almost nothing *very* well—or to completion—etc.

∞

Xmas—DC—2:10 P.M.—4110 Emery Pl NW—mostly sunny— some clouds—cold but dry—"alone" (Rain in Virginia, on way from Raleigh Springs to Charlottesville with mother and father— latter to enter hospital for operation tomorrow to "buy time" since doctors predict death soon of "renal(?)" "failure" without operation *but* less peaceful more gruesome death by bone cancer)—Cait & Miles playing with new toys—Lee & "Boo" preparing Christmas feast—me noting mentally (after "reading" M. Perloff's book on O'Hara—a wrongheaded, insufferably unknowledgeable (about what *really* goes on in "poetry" and the "making" of *it*) (& glib as well) skimming of the subject) my "favorites" of the day— 1) Meredith Monk (so happy to be preceded by her on latest Giorno "disc")   2) Sara Rudner (when she works ("dances") alone   3) Donna Dennis (she is the W. C. Williams of Am. art— about time!)   4) Ted Greenwald (the only other poet as influenced by shared "NY School" approaches to *reasons* for "making" etc. to take it somewhere "other" (me being the other to take it "other ways" etc.)   5) Jane DeLynn (whose St. Mark's reading of *Glimpses* & the typographer story overwhelmed me with the *totality* of her achievement in personalizing "fiction" "of the third kind" etc.)   6) Glen Miller (the "hipness" of rural but not redneck white America)   7) a renewed dedication to "truth in packaging" in my work and life and intentions and struggle for sainthood—

∞

Rain in the process of moving out—for real—movers come Monday—she has a place temporarily where she used to live when I met her—Broome St. & Broadway—2 office rooms—It's still pretty "amicable" but when we discuss it it's sore and trouble— Terence came up for a few days and the last night (Thurs.) he was here we all tried talking about it—no good—Rain was drunk (after a horrible few hours—12–2 A.M.?—at Mickey's—down Greenwich Street—watching the bar scene got each of us down for different reasons—Rain because she saw it as representative of "the world" to which she was returning from our relationship/ shelter—Terence because he found the place physically confining (& I suspect unexciting compared to bars he plays in and is known in) & the people unattractive & unexciting—me because the coolness & posturing—the "style"—seems so much like ripoffs of what *I've been* & yet they don't *accept me*—something like that—or I don't accept them—whatever—Terry telling me I'm crazy with my obsessions—feeling I always try within the first few moments in a place to figure out everyone's relationship to me somehow— this time "style" etc.—maybe he's right—but doesn't everyone?— he says no—he doesn't)—earlier in the evening we had enjoyed a nice "dinner" with Ted & Joan & Bill & Lin Berkson & "Josh" Bear & Donald?—nice talk nice food—we should have left it at that— but later at my kitchen table Terry & Rain & I tried to express our sense of what was going on with Rain moving out—it seemed to come down to (about the time Rain disappeared, quite drunk, to bed) *my selfishness*—!—I tried to explain through the coke & dope of the evening that I thought the relationship was heading toward a kind of nagging domesticity neither of us claimed to want—but it still ended up like I wanted to have more time & energy for acting & writing & being alone—all true too—but not the *only* "truth"—etc.

People tend to look at the light outside the head, and they need to look at the light inside the head—that is the hardest to get.

—*Sylvia Schuster*

My Work (Revised)

let's see ... "my work" ... hmmmm ... as always there's too much to say. I think "my work" is supposed to make "my life" somehow either last longer or mean more or both. So far, so good. Only, in retrospect ... I should never fuck with retrospect except for the purpose of entertaining myself or others (enlightening as an aspect of it, too) with stories ... raps ... uniquely precise perspectives of a consciousness etc. ... I am usually overwhelmed with the need to share what I am feeling and thinking and experiencing and learning and remembering ... and even forgetting and fucking up and fucking and etc. ... I don't know when that first started ... I tend to remember myself as close-mouthed for the most part until I turned 30 in 1972 and began expressing the impact feminism and "gay revolutionary theory and practice" were having on me, encouraged by both those movements to talk about what was going on inside me, fight the usual male reluctance etc. etc. ... I saw my actions at the time as necessary for growth and life and goodness ... later I saw them as slightly heroic ... still more recently I saw them as stupid and naive in many ways ... I'm grateful for the new directions and possibilities for my life and future they opened up but I'm sorry they made me so self-conscious and dependent on constantly sharing my insides with whoever seems kind enough to open up to them, it, etc. ... the formal aspect of my work seems to have been overshadowed by that autobiographical obsessiveness ... (I always thought I should write about myself as the subject I knew most about etc. etc.) (only before 30 it was more like descriptions of action and events, rather than direct expression of feelings, emotions, etc.—except for my hetero love writing

130

which could get pretty all of the above) ... but really, what usually attracted me to sitting down and working on some writing was the flow of words, the magic seductiveness of secret voices occurring to me or to my fingers as I typed or to the other words in their suggestiveness and sometimes subtle manipulation of my mind and heart ... I have always thought of myself as a poet, from as far back as I can remember hearing the word and understanding that it gave some sort of license for a life much more free than any I could see around me back then ... just as I always thought of myself as an activist in some seemingly eternal struggle to acquire more space for each of us to be ourselves in ... those were my first big ideas about myself and my "place" in the world ... and still are ... I only grew defensive and fell back on street jive and stances when I discovered that others who seemed to label themselves in similar ways were not always willing to grant me my space and my style and my right to call myself a "poet" or whatever and still secure my kicks the ways they might find ... these things are always difficult and sometimes stupid to talk about ... and ultimately only matter when they're happening, which isn't now ... now I'm trying to clarify some meanings about my work that I have avoided due to other intentions getting in the way when I was asked for words about what I do most and identify most with ... It is February 19, 1980, almost 4 P.M. on a bright and almost warm day in New York City (Duane and Greenwich Streets) and I have absolutely no money, in my pocket, in the bank, anywhere ... there was no water today, part of a feud going on between my landlord and some of us tenants in this century-old loft building ... I feel pretty special still, for no reason, almost 38 years old and still unable to sustain any kind of financial security for me and my 10-year-old son who I am proud of raising and his 11-year-old sister who will come to join us soon (and just left from a weekend visit in which I spent my final dollars on disco rollerskating and proved to them it wasn't so hard by doing it pretty well myself despite my fear of falling etc. & had the thrill of taking them to a brunch where I could introduce them to Gene Simmons, some rock'n'roll kiddy hero from Kiss whose face is a mystery to their friends but not to them now, and Art Garfunkel, and others similarly special to them and me because they made themselves a place to star from ... did I? ...

131

JEFF CHANDLER AND ME

I think a lot about
Jeff Chandler these days.
He was "prematurely gray"
as they used to say in
the days when he was a
bigger star than Brando
or Dean, for a while, and
I was a Jersey boy in love
with the cowboy in my soul.
He wasn't as good, or
as interesting an actor
as either of them, but then,
they became so instantly
familiar they never had
the aura of Hollywood star
the way he did. They
kind of hid from that
aspect of their obviously
grand success. While
Chandler just seemed to
do the best he could
in Westerns and overwritten
melodramas that allowed
a man, whose age we could
never even guess, to represent
some kind of heroic stature
we never saw expressed

quite that way. Brando,
as Terry Malloy, could've
walked down my street
unnoticed, with his busted
nose and eyebrow scar and
Jersey "deze" and "dozes."
And Dean looked like some
overwrought and overage
high school freak on goof
balls, nothing we hadn't
seen before, though never
quite that beautiful or
intense in retrospect.
But Chandler, doors would
have opened and ethnic
ladies with kids attached
to their chests would have
made the air hum with the
elegance of their desire for
a man like him. And me,
maybe I would have seen
yet another way for me to
fit in, just in case, who
could say, I too might
turn "prematurely gray"
some day.

TERMINAL CARE

for Max Blagg

Too proud to pop, too
hip to hop, that's me.
See, I was black back
when that was outrageous
& now is just righteous
as though Whitney Houston's
got soul; what she's got
is too hot for that old
label (once Mabel Dodge
was hip, or even Betty
Grable); no one ever saw
what made us able to be
our fearful, shy, and
friendly selves, but
only versions of some
dirty twelves they called
"the dozens" got us over;
kids who played Red Rover
stuck blades into each
other, calling all males
mother, or bro for brother.

(1983)

STOCKBROKERS OF DREAMS

Riff on the motherfucker, until you get it right, just let the mother-fucker go until you get it light, you ain't so bright no more but shit man you got a store full of merchandise somewhere back there in your heart, so just start the motherfucking sale and wail on the memories of a life most of these white mice would die from before they even set sail—bail—male—jailhouse rock and cunt and cock and coke and stoke those reefer fires that lit the brush in your brain and the smoke still remains to haunt your synapses with relapses of memory loss and tossing and turning all night, dee wop bleeda dee wa dee, I see.

My love, my first love, music, is life, was, is soundtrack and stimulating exercise and erotic substitution and memories and the way we were and what is it now is it nothing? I want you I need you I uh huh love you, with all my hararahararaheart uh ho-o-o-old me tight through the night in the still of I can't forget when we met who is you is it her or her or her or her or her or her what was her name so like her who I'll never get over letting go of no matter how right the reasons and her her her who has saved me so many times I should never have let go from the first time I saw her and no it wasn't her or her or her though what they each meant to me is more than they ever knew—who could tell them when all I was doing was running away, as usual—I don't need all their need all their confusion like her who can't let me go and can't let me go any further either without the total security of money and changes I can't make this late or can I you and why do you think it all has to be erotic with me just because it always has? and those men, give me a break, it was just a way of getting around the women

135

and their breaking my heart which you could never do because no matter what I wrote at the time I'm so straight and into the female body it would make you give up if you could see into the sensuality of my soulfulness and yes I miss the blackness that is mine and I abandoned in the accusations of those perilous times we call the '60s but were really epitomized in '70-1-2-3-4 when we closed the door on that dream of our Martin Luther Kings and the wings of our hearts wrapped around us in protective posturing until the swings of public hate and elation could subside—meanwhile, we did abide by the rules of rock'n'roll and tossed our souls onto the turntables of *Bus Stops* and Betty Grables and Greta Garbos and MMs and BBs and MBs and JDs—oh those "we"'s we cultivated in the gardens of our own Candymans—I mean, the teen queen rivalries that even gangs could not embody—we were mean—sure—to ourselves when we grew up to be the stockbrokers of dreams we thought we shared in common but went broke trying to sustain—the train to glory got derailed and we failed to find a home where we all could belong—I don't know, I'm awful tired, ain't you? So, where do we go from here Desiree? Up on the roof? Under the boardwalk? Downtown? On Broadway? Out on the street tonight? In my room? New York New York? I remember *Irene* Kral singing with an early Maynard Ferguson band at a time when big bands and their singers were meaningless to most—what am I, the host of minor memories I once thought grandiose? Or, is my life a toast to the most overlooked and underrated thrills and chills of winning without a contest being declared in the foist place—I mean there was no race except what it means to be human & there was never any home but the poem...

BROTHER CAN YOU SPARE A RHYME?

Once upon a time
I could rhyme
anything, but
thought it was
a cheap trick,
like being born
with a big dick
and using it
to get ahead
in Hollywood.

I would never do that.

Or like those old
cowboy movies
where the hero
always wore a white hat,
and the bad guys black.
That seemed to be
a California perception
of what looked good
on a handsome man.

Back East white was
the color for dairy queens
and guys so rich they
were terminally passive.

Black was the color
for the kind of men
who wouldn't have
known what a den
is for, or ever bore
us with their lack
of passion.
The hottest women
wore black, and
the classiest,
the saddest,
the smartest.

White and black,
now and then,
me and you,
what'll we do
about all we know
to be no longer true,
and yet still be truthful
so we can survive
these new dark ages, huh?

Maybe, you can go
home again
if you're willing to
take responsibility for
what you find there.

Even the air
is tired from what we've
all been through,
the scare
we've all been talking to
when we talk to each other
and discover
we're all a lot more
careful in the ways
we own our lives.
Some people say
there's an art to that—
yeah, the art of compromise.

KNOW

Gertrude Stein
wine
I don't know
I think they've lost their glow
for me.
See, I haven't been able to
drink either one for years now.
How did I know?
I mean, what to keep and
what had to go—
Like all those William Saroyan and
William C. Williams tomes—
those little homes I grew up in
even if I was already grown
when I first started reading them.
J. W. Dant bourbon was the thing
I liked the most.
Toasting is what blacks called
rapping back in the old days
before it became a part of the music biz.
The Wiz was an underrated movie,
says D.M., as he produces another
amazing TV show, buys and sells horses,
makes his BMW go with me in it
and I still owe him several big ones.
The man's a genius, says his agent,
after he tells me "your eyes glow,"

and all I know is my heart has broken
like those horses they send out too soon
to compete in races they can't win yet.
Only I ain't no horse,
and I been out there for years,
they didn't just send me out too early.
Although—
Hey, what do I know?

SECRET LOVE

What secret? Anybody who knows me knows I love you, and that I still love Van Morrison's songs and William Saroyan's books and Veronica Lake's movies and Thelonious Monk's genius and Alex Trebec and *Jeopardy* and the west of Ireland and Artie Shaw's last recording of "The Pied Piper Theme" and Shirley Clark's film of Warren Miller's novel *Cool World* and Celtic Thunder's version of Terence Winch's *When New York Was Irish* and *The Best Years of Our Lives* (and the movie of the same name too) and *Hard New York Days* and de Kooning's "Women" David Smith's steely constructions Marlon Brando's performance in almost everything including *Missouri Breaks* Randy Quaid's in *Midnight Express* the way Chet Baker sings "Blame It On My Youth" wait a minute this is turning into "My Favorite Things" not "secret love" because I'm lost on this one, I had plenty of "secret loves" in the '50s when my girlfriends were black and that wasn't okay, not just for my family but for the girls' families too, prejudice seems to know no prejudice, but the last time I had a secret love it wasn't that kind of prejudice that kept it secret, after I wrote about it I was still too embarrassed to read what I wrote in public back in the mid-eighties when I fell in love with "God" again, like when I was a kid only different, or maybe not so different, because even though back then the idea they were pushing seemed to be some white old bearded man in heaven I had a much more personal idea of a presence I could talk to as though it were my innermost, and as they say now, higher self, or maybe just the heart-filled-with-love kind of joy that I felt as a boy when I looked at the grass and thought hey, that looks great to roll around in, or at a cloud

141

passing over a nearby hill and thought some day I'll go over that hill and see what's on the other side maybe cowboys and Indians and women in old-fashioned dresses who love you for being exactly who you are, yeah, I was embarrassed to share that kind of boyish enthusiasm, that kid-like joyful love for something so difficult to understand, in fact, impossible, except as Rilke said of art, with the heart, the heart that seems to nurture that secret love of the Force that keeps it all going—not the one that finds parking spaces or gets you a job or picks out who is going to get shot in drive-bys and where the next war will break out, that ain't my secret love conception of a God, that's the working out of all our destinies in the chaos of free will at work all around and inside us, though if the biological engineers are right it might just be a matter of chemicals, and the God one is simply strong enough at times to give me the sensation of a heart filled with love, the kind of love that is measured only in infinity—there are no words to logically and graphically describe this kind of love which now that I think of it is truly secret because even in the public displays of people's idea of what their own love for their conception of their God might be it's all so much handed down or improvised on the spot ritual when what I'm talking of is going on inside and the only correlative expression that might match that is, well what else, love for others, be they our own species or what is considered living or not, it's all alive and it's all happening now and it's all— an open secret...

OKAY OKAY

Okay, you got no time for
Don Johnson or wait a minute,
who's the sexiest man on
TV, in the movies, this week,
not the president, unless you
love power and look out for
yourself and think this is the
last week of my own fortitude
in reverse of the salamander
eyes of Luis Buñuel. Give me
a break sister, this ain't no
Howard Johnson's, this is the
real thing, and like Dylan put
it, the moon ain't yellow it's
chicken. Forget it, I don't quote
nobody but Chuck Berry. Fuck
them poets and philosophers.
This is 19what and philosophy
and poetry got no place outside
school and inside school nobody gives a shit anyway.
Hey, today, what you need is
a little feedbag full of extra
potent vitamins and minerals
and a subscription to a health
magazine and a consumer magazine and a how to get along

with yourself and your mate
and your boss and your fate
magazine. Only, only, only, whatever
happened to Life. Life, it's
a magazine. What's the word?
Thunderbird. Okay okay, forget
the way it all rhymes, because
that's just a silly way of
saying—TOMORROW ASSHOLE!

WALK ON THE WILD SIDE

I'm so dependent on what other people think about me.
That's not the way I want to be.
I don't want to be like Laurence Harvey in
Walk on the Wild Side either. I only saw it
because it was the first time Jane Fonda played a whore.
That was long before the Viet Nam war—
or not, that wasn't a war, I forgot, Congress never
declared war on anybody in that one, that was—
what? What was that one? Not a "police action"—
that was the Korean War—it's funny isn't is,
how we're allowed to call them wars after they're over—
well, they're never really over, anyway—
I can't remember anything about that movie—
except Jane Fonda was almost as young as I was then,
and she was beautiful in this fragile sexy
teenage woman kind of way that she isn't today—
somewhere in there she turned from fragile to brittle,
the kind of distinctions real poets love to play with
but not before they throw out a lot of obviously
intelligent and imaginatively deep images so that
everyone will know it's poetry—and smart poetry
which is why I stopped doing that a long time ago
except now and then just to slow down the pace
of the ideas that always race through my mind
when it's time to write a poem which for me is
any and all the time because you see I'm a poet
and I can always make it rhyme just like the

rappers do, only middle-aged white poets ain't
supposed to, they're supposed to write about
how the rocks are talking to them tonight in
the muffled tones of their ex-wife which
implies a marriage to the earth that has been
broken up, only, when the rocks talk to me they
say stuff like what up honky homey? or whoa,
you see that stone, check her out, or, hey man,
it's okay, you're gonna make it through today
and come tonight you'll be all right no matter
what they say, you are just as much who you
were meant to be as we are brother, and the
earth is our mother too, hey someday you
might be a rock yourself like you
thought you were in 1956—
when the colored girls *did* go
"doo, da doo, da doo"—

Sometimes I Can Be a Pain in the Ass

1. You'd probably recognize him. A lot of people do. They just don't know from where. Most people think they went to high school with him, or met him at a party. "Hey, I'm Jim. We met at Carol and Bob's, remember? You were with the wife and kids. No? That wasn't you? I'm so sorry. I was sure that was you." Or just, "Where do I know you from?" But he never presumed to tell them.

2. People who move to cities to live, want to be noticed, or at least want some human contact that's sexy. People move to the suburbs for lawns, yards, more space.

3. John McCormack influenced Louis Armstrong. The first great genius of jazz said the Irish-born tenor had "beautiful phrasing." McCormack became a citizen in 1919. Fifteen hundred graduating naval trainees sang "Mother MacCree" to him, followed by the national anthem and three cheers for this newest citizen of the USA. Blaise Cendrars wrote *Easter in New York* from December 1911 to May 1912.

4. Pain destroys everything, except pain. Feeling abandoned by God, I still pray out of habit, and this habit saves me from complete despair. And then my wife and baby appear, in my dream, in my waking thought, in my hospital room and for a moment it all makes sense. Life is love and love is unconditional commitment to the happiness of the loved one(s). This saves me more deeply than any prayer, because it is the ultimate prayer.

147

5. Neilson compares me to Eliot—the unexpected rhymes, the latent Catholicism. When in pain, this means, literally, *nothing*. Books are meaningless, extraneous illusions; nonsense, pointless, stupid wastes of effort. As are movies, art, music, lovers, pasts, futures, ideas, revelations, epiphanies, truth. The only truth is *pain*. The only idea is relief. The only relief is less pain.

6. Crossing at the light at Fourth Street and Santa Monica Boulevard, in Santa Monica, in 1987 (I can't remember the month or season since it was just another sunny/smoggy day), Denise Bratton recognized me. We stopped to talk, and during the conversation she said, "Michael, the world has changed a lot. There's no admiration for the struggle any more."

7. Bing Crosby was like a member of the family when I was a boy. I was born at the beginning of World War Two, when Bing was in the home stretch of a popular peak that had lasted a decade or more. A young Frank Sinatra was vying for his crown, and in many ways was proving to be more popular, at least among young women. But Bing was still on top. *White Christmas,* his bestselling recording—which would remain the all-time bestselling record for another fifty years—had just come out. It was a good time for my family too.

8. The great writing is: Villon—who I would not have known had not John Ashbery compared my writing to his—or St. John of the Cross and his *Dark Night of the Soul,* which I discovered on my own as a teenager alone in the vestibule of Our Lady of Sorrows church in South Orange, New Jersey, where they had a rack in those days, the late 1950s, with paperback books for sale, approved by the Bishop, the Cardinal, the Church, and despite their imprimatur the pages of St. John lured me into what I read as a justification, or at least release, for my adolescent frustration into the life of exquisite decadence on the road to transcendent beatitude. Villon and St. John, the first "Beats" of my literary heart. St. John through my head, Villon through my compulsion to list my legacy, my testament of notorious achievement, to record my way into literary history before I knew how or why not.

9. I don't sing so well, but I have a story to tell and it came to me in song—the title was "Where Do We Belong?"—My grandfather

came from Galway, a crossroads called Tallyho—I went back for a visit, not so long ago—It broke my heart to see where where where where did we start? In Ballyanger, or something like that, I went to a shop run by a man named Walsh, the grandson of the man who wrote *The Quiet Man* stories. It was a good store for presents. The people said "betther" for "better" and "ahind" for "behind" as in "left ahind," and "oh it's desperate." In Dublin I called Paul Brady, a friend of a friend, but he wasn't home, so I drove straight back to Galway, where I was.

10. She had the most perfectly formed female body he had ever seen. So naturally she hated it. That was in 1989.

11. "Everything is perfect on the street again, the world is permeated with roses of happiness all the time, but none of us know it. The happiness consists in realizing that it is all a great strange dream."—Jack Kerouac

12. Pain erases everything but pain. All priorities are reordered. Life becomes *pain*—addressing it, relieving it, accepting it. God was Love—now he's Pain. Despair is how the mind feels pain. Those animated images of gloom and doom are the pain points of the drug's reaction: a thousand points of pain no drug can alleviate. Unbearable pain—born. The only response to pain is—habit: the ritual of daily communion with living. Though unbearable pain evokes nothing but death. Thank God the habitual is the last to die.

13. I see it with a clarity I've never had before. I was never completely committed to any marriage, any woman before. Always with an ace up my sleeve: another woman, my writing, reputation, fantasies. But this is it! Total commitment. I see it clearly—the most important thing in life is my marriage and my children—my love for my wife and my baby, my grown children and the babies they will have. "My wife"—for the first time I mean it. No other woman in my heart or fantasies! I weep with relief I am so full of gratitude for her presence in my life and our baby boy's—their smiles, their soft skins, their eyes shining into mine, even their frustration and impatience, the intensity of their needs. I love them for it all and want nothing but to be there for them in any way I can. I

weep at the acceptance of my fate, it is theirs. Is it the drugs? The pain? The epiphany of helplessness as I lie there in that hospital bed, fed morphine intravenously...

VENICE CA (1980S)

1

The director had a lot of charisma. He had been an actor. He had
a large nose and intense and beautiful eyes and a full head of hair
that seemed stylishly unruly. He had been making his living as a
screenwriter, but was ready to direct. He had two projects. One
was about a sort of sado-masochistic love affair, in which he
wanted to star a relative newcomer, Mickey Rourke, who had a
very small role in *Body Heat* and damn near stole the movie. So he
was hot and already somebody. I supposedly was too, though for
not such an obvious reason.

The movie the director wanted me to star in was about two
women and a man in their late thirties. One woman would be my
character's wife, or girlfriend, and he wanted my wife at the time
to play her. She was a well-known and much honored actress and
could help sell the movie he thought. The other female role was of
a housewife, with two small kids, who my character was supposed
to have an affair with. He wanted the woman I was having an
affair with at the time to play her.

My wife had been nominated for an Oscar. The other actress
had won one of Canada's version of the Oscar. She was blonde.
My wife was a redhead. I didn't know how the director sensed the
situation, but they were both ambitious enough to want to take
advantage of it, and so was he. I was thrilled. I was going to star in
a Hollywood movie. At last. I'd fantasized about that since I was a
kid but done little to accomplish it until now.

I'd starred in a few student and avant-garde little films, as more or less myself, and in two horrible low-budget horror movies, in which I too was horrible. But this was my big break. The director only had to convince the producer, an Englishman, who lived way up on top of Mulholland Drive in an enormous mansion. We took the director's old Mercedes up to meet him and then all went down to Chinatown for dinner and to talk.

I wore the customized leather sport jacket my wife had bought me in Rome while she was there making a movie. I didn't have to wear my glasses all the time back then, and my hair was mostly all there and still had a lot of darkness to it with some gray mixed in. I was slim and cocky and ready. When I got up to play the jukebox I heard the director stage whisper to the producer to watch how the women checked me out. And they did. I was beside myself with glee, but covered it with the cool I had manufactured to live up to the image I had created to hide behind, without knowing that's what I was doing. Why should I know it, it worked. Most of the time.

The only thing I objected to was that I thought Rourke, whose work I already admired, would be better for the role they were casting me for, and me for the role they were casting him for. The other role was more elegant, more cool, more handsome and suave and all the things I believed I was inside and only needed the chance to show the world I could be. The role they cast me for was of the working class bad boy, the cool dude, the carny who steals the housewife away from her complacency and changes hers, and his and his wife's lives. As was happening in my real life.

Meanwhile, Hollywood was going through a periodic shake-out. It was the mid-80s and suddenly the "Brat Pack" was happening and movies were being rewritten to skew younger and edginess was out and gimmickry was in and the financing disappeared for the movie. But the other one got made. It took a few years, and someone else directed it. By the time it came out Rourke was already a star of sorts, and I was working on the last of the '80s TV shows based on the *Dallas* model, only mine was set in a department store and died after one season. My wife and I had divorced, the other actress had moved on.

The director had told me, at that first meeting, that he knew me as a poet, had read a poem of mine about the Jersey shore in which I wrote that "we" used to jump into cars and cruise over to a nearby town and jump out with baseball bats to hit Jews in the head and then jump back in and return to our enclave. I pointed

152

out that the Jewish guys from our neighborhood went with us, so it wasn't exactly anti-Semitic.

But then he told me he had grown up in that nearby town, and in fact had been caught in the head one night by a baseball bat from one of those guys in one of those cars, and then laughed, I wasn't sure if he was putting me on, or playing with me, or getting some kind of twisted revenge. When the movie died, I thought maybe it had all been set up to pulverize my ego.

2

Several years later, now nearing fifty, I was invited by the director to a screening of a new movie of his. He had directed a few movies, and a cable TV series was still on the air. He was successful. I was curious. I went to the screening wondering why I was there. Then the movie started, and it took a few scenes before I realized it was the movie I was supposed to star in, only with a different name, and the characters now in their twenties, and the housewife no longer with children, or maybe even married, I was too distracted to notice.

The actress who played her was very sexy. The guy who played my role was much younger, of course, and bigger, built up. But, I thought to myself, not as cool as I thought I once was. And then it hit me. I would never get to play that role, or any like it. The bad boy roles I thought I could define forever, because I thought I had been what these actors were trying to copy, were forever out of my reach. I was too old. There was no turning back. The fantasy that had sustained me in movie theaters for almost half a century was over. I was too old to ever play that role now.

I missed most of the rest of the movie, fighting dizziness and tears. When I exited, the director stopped me to ask what I thought. I had trouble answering, even talking, but somehow blurted out: "Why did you invite me?" He said, "I wanted you to see that guy I found. He walked in cold, no agent, no scheduled appointment, and the minute I saw him, I said, that's Lally. Not as cool maybe, but he had that kind of romantic innocent tough guy softy thing going on, just like you. I thought you'd dig him."

3

I saw the director one more time. He had an annual Christmas party at his Venice house, until he got so successful he moved to a much wealthier enclave in Santa Monica, where I had been living when we first met. He invited me and I went. I brought my kids, because he had two himself, though his were girls and mine were a boy and girl. I was glad I did, because a dark-haired beauty was cruising me from across the room all night and I wasn't wearing my glasses, to look cool of course, and couldn't see who she was. My kids told me later it was Madonna in a dark tresses phase.

At one point in the party my host called me to join him and some other men. I recognized some as rock'n'roll stars or film actors, the others I didn't know. After he had gathered a group of about maybe a dozen of us—it was a big party, we weren't even missed—and had us form a circle, he told us all to look down. We did. And every one of us was wearing some kind of boot with a pointed toe, not cowboy boots, closer to the Beatle boots I was still wearing, originals I had refused to give up since before they were even associated with any Beatles. Our host said, as we all looked back up, "We're all from Jersey."

I didn't see him much again, though when I did I was always happy to. He was a happy guy, who was always full of praise for whatever project he was working on, and he had almost made me a star. But I stopped wearing the boots, gave my customized leather to my son, started wearing my glasses so I could see who was looking at me, or even if they really were.

The movie I didn't star in more or less bombed. The actors in it went on to other things, but never made it really big. Meanwhile, my ex-wife ended up waiting tables for a while, and me driving a limo for stars and agents and producers and directors I once worked with, or almost did. The other actress got married and had a child and works steadily. I don't know where any of them are now. I'm back in Jersey, married to the woman who has become the love of my life. I feel lucky to have found her before it was too late. We have a beautiful two-year-old boy we adore, whose theatrical passion and intensity, and crazy creative manipulativeness keeps me laughing at my karma.

LOOSE CANON

Bing Crosby singing "Galway Bay"
Glenn Miller's band singing and playing "I Got a Gal in
     Kalamazoo-zoo-zoo-zoo"
Johnny Mercer singing "Ac-cen-tu-ate the Positive"
Veronica Lake and Alan Ladd in *The Blue Dahlia*
Jimmy Cagney and the Dead End Kids in *Angels with Dirty Faces*
The Third Man
Marlon Brando in *On the Waterfront*
Blackboard Jungle
Elvis Presley singing falsetto on his Sun recording of "Blue
     Moon"
Listening to a recording of Johnny Ace singing "Forever My
     Darling" and knowing he had already killed himself
The first time I listened to Chuck Berry's lyrics for "Maybelline"
     and then later for "Roll Over, Beethoven"
Aaron Copland's music for Martha Graham's dance piece
     Appalachian Spring on black-and-white TV
Seeing the movie *Marty* the first time, when I was in 8th grade
Nat King Cole singing "Mona Lisa" on his black-and-white
     "black and white" show
"In the Still of the Night" as the soundtrack of the movie of my
     life in the summer of 1956 down the Jersey shore
The sound of Johnny Mathis singing "It's Not for Me to Say"
     while falling in love with a girl who told me her father
     wouldn't let me date her because we came from "two

different worlds" meaning she was rich and we were not

Frankie Lyman and the Teenagers singing "I'm Not a Juvenile
      Delinquent" in the movie *Rock, Rock, Rock!* when he was
      supposedly the same age as I was at the time, thirteen

The Broadway cast album of *West Side Story*

"Lieutenant Cable" singing "You Have To Be Carefully Taught"
      in the movie of *South Pacific*

Billie Holiday's voice singing anything, especially "Strange Fruit"

Ditto for Frank Sinatra, especially on the album *Only the Lonely*

The sound of Miles Davis' trumpet

Ahmad Jamal's versions of outdated corny tunes on his LP
      Poinciana and the impact it had on my own piano style

Seeing photographs of Rodin's sculpture of lovers

Listening to Nina Simone play and sing "Summertime" at The
      Village Gate in 1959 when it was a basement club under
      a rundown hotel and I was too young to get in so I sat on
      the grating in the sidewalk over whatever was behind the
      bandstand and got drunk on cheap wine and felt inspired
      by both her singing and playing and four years later in
      Spokane, Washington, did my version of hers, minus the
      singing, on a TV talent-contest show that was rigged
      upfront so the daughter of a locally powerful businessman
      would win and we got paid to pretend to compete

The Miles Davis album *Kinda Blue,* especially "So What"

Miles' solo on the vendor's song ("Strawberries") on *Porgy and
      Bess*

The way Bill Evans played piano, and the impact when I first
      heard him on his "Waltz for Debbie" with Scott LaFaro
      on bass and later performing his solo composition "Peace
      Piece"

Thelonious Monk's composing and piano playing, especially on
      his " 'Round Midnight" and me trying to figure out the
      chords he used and realizing the magnitude of his genius

Charles Mingus' bass playing, compositions, and autobiography
      Beneath the Underdog, and then seeing the black-and-white
      documentary of his harassment by landlords and
      Marshals and an indifferent world breaking his and my
      heart

The Dark Night of the Soul by St. John of the Cross

The City Lights broadside of "Second April" by Bob Kaufman

Diane DiPrima's poem series *Thirteen Nightmares*

156

50 Poems by e. e. cummings

Leaves of Grass by Walt Whitman

Lambert, Hendricks, and Ross singing Jon Hendricks' lyrics to
Charlie Parker's "Now's the Time"

The first time I read James Joyce's *Portrait of the Artist as a Young
Man* in 1960, and each time I've read it since

Thomas Merton's *Seven Storey Mountain*

The first time I heard a recording of John Coltrane, and
everything of his I heard after that, but especially when I
went to hear him at The Village Gate in 1960 and he
played "My Favorite Things" on the alto sax with a
combo that included two basses

Fyodor Dostoevsky's *Notes from Underground*

Bogart and Bergman in *Casablanca*

Reading William Saroyan's first collection of short stories, *The
Daring Young Man on the Flying Trapeze* for the first time
and then his novella *Tracy's Tiger,* both books altering my
perception of myself in the world and going on to read
everything he ever wrote no matter how self-indulgent or
unintentionally pretentious and continuing to be inspired
and encouraged by his example

Reading *The Subterraneans* and *Lonesome Traveler* by Jack Kerouac
when they first came out

Shirley Clark's film of Warren Miller's novel *Cool World*

On first reading a translation of the *Tao Te Ching*

William Goldman's first novel, *Temple of Gold,* written when he
was twenty-four

Jack Kerouac reading his work on *The Steve Allen Show*

Seeing the original black-and-white independent film *David and
Lisa* when it first came out

Barbra Streisand's versions of forgotten tunes, especially her
slowed-down rendition of "Happy Days Are Here Again"
on her first album

Justine by Lawrence Durrell

Danny Lyons' photographs in *The Bikeriders*

Going to see Federico Fellini's *8½* when it first came out, with
my first wife and my first "intellectual" friends, afraid I
wouldn't "get" it, and only a few scenes into it identifying
completely with the filmmaker's creative subjectivity

Reading a used copy of the first Evergreen edition of Samuel
Beckett's *Waiting for Godot* and then going on to read

157

everything he ever wrote and being inspired by it all
The Notebooks of Malte Laurids Brigge by Rainer Maria Rilke
Tales by LeRoi Jones
A Season in Hell by Arthur Rimbaud
Frank O'Hara's *Lunch Poems* discovered and initially dismissed by
      me at the home of my first intellectual friend, Roy
      Harvey, outside Spokane, Washington in 1964 as too
      "elitist" but I continued to reread them until in 1972 they
      finally broke through my defensiveness to open me up to
      not only the intricacies of his craft and the uniqueness of
      his approach to constructing a poem and his love of
      words and all they can do but to my own love affair with
      the language I knew
My first wife turning me on to Bob Dylan's "The Times They Are
      A-changin' " after I told her I'd met him in the Village
      earlier and thought he was a phony, then hearing
      everything else he'd written and recorded and being
      "blown away" by it all
Eric Dolphy playing anything, but most amazingly his flute solo
      on "You Don't Know What Love Is" and bass clarinet on
      Monk's "Epistophy" on the posthumous album *Last Date*
Seeing the Beatles in *A Hard Day's Night* and not only getting
      over my anger at the British invasion horning in on my
      freelance career as a club musician, but wanting to *be* a
      Beatle
Coltrane's seminal recording, *A Love Supreme*
Gary Snyder reading poems from his book *Rip Rap* in a fifteen-
      minute black-and-white educational film segment on TV
      in 1966
Vanessa Redgrave and David Warner in *Morgan*
The first time I read *Paterson* by William Carlos Williams and felt
      reassured as well as energized by his brand of New
      Jersey/American language
The Tale of Genji by Lady Murasaki
Reading the Jacobean play *'Tis a Pity She's a Whore* by John Ford
The first time I read James Wright's poems "The Blessing" and
      "Autumn Comes to Martins Ferry, Ohio"
Laurence Sterne's seminal novel *Tristram Shandy*
Cane by Jean Toomer
Winesburg, Ohio by Sherwood Anderson
Coming out of a "modern" group exhibit of sculptors—at the

Chicago Art Institute and feeling deeply disappointed
until I looked up and saw a sculpture by David Smith,
whose work was not included in the exhibit, and who has
had a regrettable influence on bad "modern" public
sculpture, but all of whose work has mesmerized and
inspired and enlightened me whenever I see it in person
Watching Ray DiPalma perform in several plays at the University
of Iowa, from Jarry to Pinter, 1966–68, and then in New
York in 1981, watching him in my own one-act play, *Four
Grown Men*
And Ray DiPalma's approach to what would become known as
"language-centered writing" when we first were friends
and watching it develop into something uniquely personal
Robert Slater's Midwest hipster's perspective in his poetry and
advice
Otis Redding's in-concert recording of "Try a Little Tenderness"
Jimi Hendrix's "Are You Experienced" and all his guitar work
Vladimir Mayakovsky's poem "A Cloud in Trousers"
Janis Joplin's voice singing "Summertime" on her first LP *Cheap
Thrills*, hitting me in the heart as it wailed out of a hippie
party in a country farmhouse on the outskirts of Iowa
City in 1968
Kurasawa's black-and-white film *The Seven Samurai*
T. S. Eliot's "The Lovesong of J. Alfred Prufrock"
On first encountering the art of Francis Picabia
Ditto the poetry and prose of Blaise Cendrars
And ditto again the art of Sylvia Schuster
After dismissing *The Sonnets* by Ted Berrigan as secondhand
(having recognized favorite lines by others in them), and
then meeting and arguing with him over them, and
impressed with his responses, rereading them and
realizing how revolutionary and extraordinary they, and
all his poems, are
The Awakening by Kate Chopin
Bernardo Bertolucci's *The Conformist*
Soap by Francis Ponge
Mumbo Jumbo by Ishmael Reed
Relistening to Aretha Franklin's recording of "You Make Me Feel
Like a Natural Woman" under the influence of feminism
Discovering Bonnard's paintings at the Phillips Gallery in
Washington, DC

Instructed by Sylvia Schuster to sit in a room full of Mark
Rothko paintings in the same gallery until I got them, and
after an hour and twenty-odd minutes having a spiritual
epiphany
Peter Schejdahl taking me to see the art of Eva Hesse in a Soho
gallery for the first time around 1970
Rereading Jack Kerouac's *Big Sur* and *Desolation Angels* and then
reading for the first time his *Vanity of Duluoz* and the
posthumous complete edition of *Visions of Cody*
Doug Lang's novel *Freaks*
Encountering Bruce Andrews' poetry after meeting him in The
Community Bookstore in Washington, DC, which I was
co-running at the time, 1971, and arguing over "new
jazz" and the "New York School" poetry scene etc. and his
going on to share his "language-centered" work and
theories with me and showing me how a lot of my early
work fit the same theories
The poems of Ed Cox
Reading the first installment of Joe Brainard's long list poem, "I
Remember" and looking forward to more
Seeing a Joseph Cornell box for the first time
Marlon Brando in Bertolucci's *Last Tango in Paris*
Martin Scorcese's *Mean Streets*
Sitting through Marcel Ophuls' documentary film *The Sorrow and
the Pity* and not wanting it to end
Van Morrison's "Listen to the Lion" and his intuitive musicality
on everything he ever performed or recorded
John Lennon's "A Working Class Hero Is Something to Be" and
everything else he ever wrote, performed, drew or said
Seeing Michaelangelo's *Slaves,* first in photographs, then in
person
James Schuyler's long poem "Hymn to Life" and then later seeing
my name in his last long poem "The Morning of the
Poem"
Hearing John Ashbery read his poems in a series I was also
reading in at the Smithsonian Institution in 1972 and
finally getting not only the profound wit of it, but by
hearing each word as a note in a free jazz solo I got what
he was talking about too
A few years later finding a unique inspiration in his *Three Poems*
Marvin Gaye performing his "What's Goin' On"

160

Early Morning Wind by Dale Herd

A Quincy History by James Haining

Seeing Marlon Brando in a revival house showing of *A Streetcar Named Desire* for the *first* time when I was 31

On my first trip to Europe at 32 seeing Gaudi's architecture in Barcelona

Running into Ted Greenwald on the street in Manhattan shortly after I moved back there in 1975 and noting how seriously and respectfully he spoke of his poetry, moving me to reread it and discover the unique way he had created to use words as a dadaist sculptor might have used found objects to create a recognizable yet mysteriously alternate reality

Seeing Richard Foreman's play *Rhoda in Potatoland* starring Kate Manheim at the theater in his loft

Coming around a corner in the Metropolitan Museum of Art and walking into a series of Robert Motherwell paintings inspired by the Spanish Civil War and getting them

Hearing Terry Riley's "Composition in C" or whatever it's called performed by him at the old Kitchen in Soho

Opening the window to our Duane Street loft in what would unfortunately become known as Tribeca and suddenly realizing that not just us, but everyone in that still "bohemian" (pre-DeNiro et al.) neighborhood was, at that moment, playing the Philip Glass album *North Star*

Listening to Charlmagne Palestine play one of his percussionary piano pieces at the old Customs House in downtown Manhattan surrounded by Reginald Marsh murals

Watching Sara Rudner dance solo at St. Mark's and illuminate the stages of a woman's life from birth to death without making it trite or obvious, in fact no one I was with saw it that way, but I was so deeply moved I wanted to jump up and shout "Marry me!"

Rain Worthington's concert at The Kitchen in 1978, where she played her compositions based on meticulously intricate patterns that she put together and memorized bit by bit since she didn't read or write music and had no musical training or background, the sound simple and pure and reminding me of a contemporary Satie, only she was a true musical "primitive" or "outsider" which the downtown academically trained scene unfortunately

dismissed for exactly the qualities that made her work
unique

Jane DeLynn reading her story "Glimpses" at St. Mark's in 1979

Hearing Blondie's "Heart of Glass" on a jukebox in a truckstop
while on the road and feeling like it was somehow a
shared victory for our entire downtown neighborhood
back in Manhattan

Seeing a Willem de Kooning painting from his *Women* series in
person for the first time

On first seeing a Philip Guston painting of giant cigarette butts

On first reading Kenward Elmslie's play *City Junket*, and then
years later seeing it performed (I was house manager)
with Red Groome sets at a midtown theater in an old
church, despite the bad reviews, the audience was always
full of the cream of New York's creative community and I
was happy to be a witness to it

Celtic Thunder's recording of Terence Winch's "When New York
Was Irish" and everything else Winch has written or
performed

Seeing the premiere of Robert Wilson's *Einstein on the Beach* at
the Metropolitan Opera House at Lincoln Center,
standing room only, with people I knew from downtown
hanging off the box seats, all of us mesmerized for hours
by Wilson's vision

Getting out of a sickbed, with an intense fever, to support my
friend Karen Allen in an Actors Studio performance of
Monday After the Miracle, William Gibson's follow-up to
The Miracle Worker, but this time about the adult Helen
Keller, played by Karen, and watching her glow so fiercely
from within her muted blind character that Ellen Burstyn
and John Hurt seemed like amateurs overwhelmed by her
strength and determination and presence, as the real life
characters they were attempting to portray must have
been by Keller herself

Seeing David Lynch's film *Eraserhead* when it first came out and
somehow identifying with the lead character, or at least
his surroundings

Seeing Frank Gehry's house in Santa Monica for the first time

Bruno Ganz's performance in the film *Knife in the Head*

Being surprised and amazed at the incredibly powerful and
controlled sound that came out of my daughter Caitlin

162

when she sang classical pieces for her college senior
thesis, and then later at an art show by her class, being
impressed most by a painting that I wanted to buy it was
so unique, and finding out it was hers
Finally reading Henry Miller and being surprised and moved by
his spiritual insights in books like *Sexus* and *Big Sur* etc.
Watching the Stephen Sondheim musical *Sunday in the Park with
George* on video and being moved to tears for art and
artists and for myself and the struggle to do the work no
matter what
Merril Gilfillan's *Magpie Rising*
Drugstore Cowboy directed by Gus Van Sant
Seeing my son Miles perform with other dancers a piece he
created for his college senior thesis and being humbled by
his wit and originality and genuine artistry, and later
feeling the same way about his bass playing, particularly
the music he created to back my poetry on a recording
that never got released
Rereading *Last Exit to Brooklyn* and getting it this time
Then seeing Jennifer Jason Leigh in the film version and not long
afterward as a different kind of hooker in *Miami Blues* and
realizing she's the Brando of her generation
On discovering Lee Miller's photographs and life story
On a first date with a beautiful black woman seeing *Field of
Dreams* in a movie theater in Westwood, where it had just
premiered, and thinking it had too many flaws, especially
the absence of the greats of the "Negro Leagues" as
though the afterlife were segregated, when suddenly, at
the very end, as Kevin Costner's character gets to play
catch with his long gone but still young father who
doesn't even know it's his son, I hear this explosion of
sobs and realize it's me and I can't stop, and no way to
explain to my date what's happening except that I never
mourned the death of my father until that moment
Wim Wenders' film *Wings of Desire*
Watching Vanessa Redgrave act in *Howards End* and wanting to
jump up in the theater and shout "Vanessa Redgrave is
God" or something equally silly and impetuous but
heartfelt
And then seeing *Remains of the Day* and realizing how great
Hopkins is, not to mention Emma Thompson, but

especially him in that moment when she goes to take the
book from his arms

Hearing and seeing Kurt Cobain perform "Smells Like Teen
Spirit" the first time

Reading a love poem of John Godfrey's to a bookstore audience
in Westwood one night and realizing not only how great
his work is, I always thought that, but how transcendently
universal it is, in ways I only dreamt of being

Natalie Portman and Jean Reno in Luc Besson's *The Professional*

Watching Sharon Stone kick ass in *Casino*

The Tim Robbins–directed film of *Dead Man Walking,* everything
about it including one of my favorite actors, Ray Barry,
but especially the work of Sean Penn and Susan
Sarandon, both of whose work is always good, often
incredible, but in this film they went beyond anything
they had ever done before

Simon Pettet's book of Rudy Burkhart sayings and photographs
Talking Pictures

After years of dismissing the art of R. B. Kitaj when I
encountered it in reproductions, usually in some obscure
arty book of poems, I finally ran into one of his canvases
at the Metropolitan Museum in NYC and was stopped
cold by the inclusiveness of his technique and the power
of his commitment

Being turned on to reruns of *Northern Exposure* by my wife and
realizing TV could be as good as the best movies and
books and music and paintings, though I intuitively knew
that, back when I was a kid and Sid Caesar and Imogene
Coca had me writhing on the floor in uncontrollable
laughter, or Jackie Gleason had me mesmerized by a
talent so obviously big in every way I could only marvel at
it, or John Cassavetes brought his unique talent to his
starring role as the Beat, jazz pianist and part-time
detective *Johnny Staccato,* or David Milch brought his
unique writing skills to *Hill Street Blues* and *NYPD Blue*
on which I got to play an artist and pay homage to Joe
Brainard and Sylvia Schuster

And more I'm sure I can't remember now but will as soon as this
is published

164

3

It Takes One to Know One

Stop worrying if your vision
Is new.
Let others make that decision—
They usually do.
You keep moving on.

> —Stephen Sondheim
> *Sunday in the Park with George*

If you don't say what you want, what's the sense
of writing?

> —Jack Kerouac
> *Vanity of Duluoz*

Having come to this place
I set out once again
On the dark and marvelous way
From where I began:
Belief in the love of the world,
Woman, spirit, and man.

> —Muriel Rukeyser
> "This Place in the Ways"

NEWARK POEM

I never made it to Morocco, Paris, Tangiers,
Tokyo, Madrid. I just live here, in Newark
& wait, for Morocco, Paris, Tangiers, Tokyo
& Madrid to make it to me, here in Newark.

FAMILY VALUES

family values family values family values
that phrase has the same rhythmic resonance
as light my fire light my fire light my fire
which, I guess, is where it all began, family,
I mean around the fire, where I was not too
long ago, metaphorically and literally speaking,
visiting the land of my fathers, and finding
them, in country kitchens, where an industrial
looking but small enamel stove now sits in
what once was the fireplace in the kitchens
that warmed and often still do the entire home,
and for fuel they still use the peat, turf,
dried hunks of bog that once were dead trees
in a time when trees were almost everywhere,
that's what "kil" means in Irish I think,
tree, as in Kilkenny, the tree of, etc. etc.
or does it mean church? I forget,
but I digress, I guess, though it's all connected in my mind, especially the time they
still don't call a holocaust, or even genocide, except those in the know, it's still
referred to if at all in whatever literature
and news ever includes events that long ago,
though there are those alive whose parents
suffered through it, just like so many more
recent holocausts and genocides, I'm talking
about the Irish "famine" of the late 1840s when

there was enough food, but not enough money
in the hands of those who needed it most,
and so there are these news accounts and
personal descriptions in letters and official
documents of the time that are more than gross,
of emaciated skeleton people, entire families,
eyes and bellies distended but lifeless on
frames where the skin hardly hid the fragile
bones, discoveries of seven, thirteen, twenty
people living in homes that were little more
than twigs over mud, huddled together in their
final hours, some already dead and being
devoured by starving rats or dogs the rest
too weak to move themselves let alone the bodies,
every last leaf and blade of grass chewed up
and passed undigested, useless to stave off
but only prolonged the slow agony we see on TV now
in places like Africa where it's local clans
causing most of the grief, but in the country
I descend from it was the oppressors right
next door who defeated people who had taken care
of themselves well enough for thousands of years
but now with their land robbed and their customs
outlawed and their chances for survival reduced to
fleeing by the thousands to wherever would take them,
though none did that graciously—there were riots
in Philadelphia sounding a lot like our more recent
ones, only the targets of the rampaging mobs were
Catholics who were hung or beaten or stabbed
to death by crowds of local "patriots" saving
America from the foreign papist hordes, oh lord,
how many times must this stupid scenario be acted
out before the value of the family of man is
finally agreed upon, I am a product of the
traditional one, they say, and yet even my
mother had to go to work toward the end, when
I was the last one left, because of a recession
under a popular Republican president, in the
fabulous fucked-up '50s, so fondly remembered by
those who would have us repeat them, conveniently
forgetting how even Ike was incapable of keeping

the "military-industrial complex," as he named
it, from influencing government policy in favor
of the corporations that even then were all about
weapons and oil and chemicals, stuff they still
insist keeps us alive, refusing to admit the way
they kill, the last Zenith plant closed down,
the last car made in L.A. produced not that long
ago, the last Schwinn bicycle built only days
before, all plants that shut their doors on
American workers to go off to some so-called
foreign shore where maybe the workers are under-
paid or maybe it's just the tax breaks or who
knows what and who cares the facts are that they
try to blind us with their family values charade
while the parade of work you really get paid for
is marching lemming-like into the sea and they
blame people like you and me, because we are
single parents or the product of them, and we have
values they could never comprehend because we don't
have to defend the love we feel for all of us no
matter which side of the abortion line you're on
or what's between the legs of whoever you make
a home with, we don't insist you all be like us,
or do we? are we just as biased and narrow-minded
and so mired in our own history of excuses that
we refuse to see the value in their family ways?
do we only get real honest with people who are
into body mutilation when that's our thing or
the left-wing equivalent of right-wing bigots
or what am I trying to say? That we are one family
somewhere back far enough, and the only family value
I can think of that all families share is not starving.

LALLY'S ALLEY

I grew up in South Orange, New Jersey, in the 1940s and '50s, in a neighborhood that ran alongside the railroad tracks cutting through the middle of our town and the other towns that, like ours, bordered Newark, our local city. Our neighborhood had an A&P, a bowling alley, several new and used car lots, a candy store—with soda fountain, cigarettes, cigars, newspapers and racing forms—churches and gas stations and bars and several shops that specialized in Italian food. Our streets were full of foreign accents—Irish, Italian, and Slavic mostly—as well as the various "American" accents of their descendants and of what were then called "Negroes."

The street I grew up on started on a little hill just one house above ours and descended to cross Valley Street, which ran parallel to the railroad tracks, and then dead-ended into those tracks near a "roundhouse" for storing and turning railroad cars. As little boys we loved to watch the railroad workers disconnect the cars and push them off on to side railings or bring out others from the roundhouse, but going down there we risked being frightened by the hobos who had a camp nearby among the weeds and bushes. When we got older, we paid back the hobos, scaring them with our teenage aggression, and scaring ourselves by hopping passing trains to get to nearby towns, or jumping off on the way home. As I wrote in an early poem, "One year somebody got a plate in his head from / jumping off onto something hard like my cousins."

Eventually those trains, and the highways that ran alongside them, took me far away from South Orange. But twice I came back to live in Manhattan, only a short bus ride across the river from Newark, a distance most people I grew up with rarely if ever traveled, seeing New York City as violent, sinful, expensive, and unfriendly. Getting to know it on my own as a teenager, I argued with my friends and family about how it was a lot safer and less secretly sinful than our neighborhood, but no one ever believed me.

At any rate, I had the good luck to move back to New York in my twenties not long before my mother passed away, giving me the opportunity to visit her often in her last months, which was a gift. And then a decade later in my thirties, I again returned to New York City to live, not long before my father passed away. Visiting him was more problematic, until I discovered a formula to keep us from arguing—never talk about politics or current events, never talk about myself or my life, only ask about long gone days, before I was born, when there was nothing he could blame on me.

He was still living in South Orange, around the corner from where I grew up, in the home of one of my sisters and her policeman husband. When I'd visit, as soon as I came into the room where my father sat most of the day in front of a TV, and before he could get into interrogating me, I'd say something like "Whatever happened to Charlie Zigler?" He'd look at me for a second, as though wondering if I really cared to know, and then, unable to resist the memories, he'd say, "Charlie Zigler—he was a funny guy. Once he said about a man we knew 'He's afraid to throw a rock through the poorhouse window for fear of hitting one of his kids.'" And that would remind him of something else, and off he'd go.

It was while he reminisced that I learned things about him that made it easier for me to forgive him for his attempts to stop me from doing the things I loved, from loving the people I loved, from just being myself and happy to be. I began to understand from things he said that his Irish immigrant father had frightened him in many ways—and I could see I was like his father in a lot of those ways. But I also came to understand that he loved his father as much as his Irish immigrant mother, whom he always spoke of with devotion and an invincible respect, even when he referred to her as "a live-out maid," who, when he was a boy, often had to spend nights away in the house of the rich people she worked for.

He told me how she was the one who talked the police doctor into getting my grandfather an early retirement from the force, saving him from getting kicked off. My grandfather was still legendary, when I was growing up, as a genius at coming up with ways to avoid working. Like once, soon after they installed the first police phones, my grandfather was drinking at a neighborhood bar instead of walking his beat on the other side of the tracks up on the hill we called a "mountain." Every now and then, he'd call in from the nearest phone and when the captain at the station finally got suspicious and asked where he was, my grandfather said, "Up on the mountain, can't you hear the wind blowin' up here?" and then he blew into the phone and hung up.

Not many years later, my grandmother saw the patience of everyone he worked with running out, so she begged the police doctor to find a way to get my grandfather an early retirement before he was fired. The doctor came up with a story of a bad back because he felt sorry for my grandmother burdened with all those kids and a drunk for a husband. So my grandfather retired to the rocking chair on the porch of his house at the bottom of our street and remained a legend among the Irish in our community, especially the cops, who in later years would start their rounds by driving up our street in their police cars, giving my grandfather a little salute as he raised his bottle to them in return.

When my father passed on these stories to me before his death, the poignancy of his devotion to his mother, and his anger and disappointment toward his father, allowed me to not only better understand his anger toward me for most of my adolescence and adulthood, but also to understand some of the roots of my own anger. His stories about the days when he was a boy in the early years of the 20th century were often funny and afforded us an opportunity to laugh together, something we both welcomed. But there was always an undercurrent of disappointment in his father—the tough "mick" known as "Iron Mike" who seemed not to care much about anyone—and in himself, because despite his determination my father had failed to become the American success story he had hoped to be.

Listening to him talk, I saw the boy that he'd been, still hoping for the best, still loving his father no matter what and waiting for that love to be reciprocated. Especially when, one day, he described hiding in the shadows at the top of the stairs on nights when his mother was home, watching her and his father push back the few pieces of furniture so they and their Irish immigrant friends could dance to music my grandfather helped make on the pennywhistle or the Irish accordion. I could see how deeply my father loved them from his place in the dark at the top of the stairs with whatever other siblings were up there with him spying on the grownups.

I had no idea my grandfather played music, or even cared about it by the time I knew him. I knew my father loved music, at least some of it, and thought it was a good idea for his children to learn to play instruments to keep us out of trouble. But he had been adamant in his objections to the "jazz" I came to love, and he tried in every way he knew to thwart my ambitions to make my living playing it. He was afraid of the lifestyle that my love of jazz led me to, which he and I argued endlessly about until I finally left home in my teens to rarely come back again.

But like I said, in my thirties, just months before he died, I found myself living in New York, across the river from our New Jersey neighborhood where he still lived with one of my sisters and her policeman husband. After a few futile attempts to visit without arguing, I found a way to reconcile our differences, by leading him back into his childhood. And as an unforeseen benefit I learned about the roots of those differences. On the day he described himself as a little boy listening to his father play Irish music while his mother and their friends danced late into the night, I suddenly understood him as I understood myself, because my fondest memories of my childhood and of my father were also associated with the music in our tiny but crowded household when I was a boy in the 1940s.

There was a wide variety of music played on the radio in our house back then, from the classical station my father listened to on Sunday mornings while we were all getting ready to go to Mass, to *The Make Believe Ballroom* popular songs my two older sisters tuned into on Saturday mornings, to programs that played the Big Band swing my three older brothers were into, or comedy shows at night that featured occasional music, like Dennis Day's Irish tenor on *The Jack Benny Show*.

There were plenty of records too, those old 78s with one song on each side, like Bing Crosby's classic recording of "White Christmas" that came out in 1942, the year I was born. Bing Crosby was a big favorite in my family, largely because he was one of our own, an Irish-American. I especially loved him as a boy, because he reminded me of my father and my uncles, men who, like Bing, had come of age in the 1920s F. Scott Fitzgerald "Jazz Age." Scott and Bing were more assimilated into the American

174

mainstream than my father and most of his brothers ever were. But along with Crosby and Fitzgerald, my father and uncles shared a kind of sharp good looks and easy confidence associated in my mind with America of the 1920s.

The men in my father's family knew they were so much more a part of that time and place than their immigrant Irish parents, it gave them a lightness of tone and perception that turned everything into a joke or a song or both. I remember my uncles drunk at parties singing all kinds of tin pan alley Irish-American tunes they would supply their own words to, making fun of their "race" —as nationalities were called then. Like my Uncle Lydie singing to some popular melody: "It must have been the Irish who built the pyramids, 'cause no one else would carry all them bricks."

It was a typically Irish kind of reverse pride, the message they seemed always to be promoting: don't take yourself or anything else too seriously, because it's all apt to be pulled out from under you at any moment anyway, but on the other hand, even in our thickheadedness, we Irish are unique. My uncle Lydie was a good example of that attitude, he rarely seemed to me as a boy to take anything very seriously. Having spent part of his boyhood in reform school for some transgression I never learned the exact nature of, but assumed had something to do with stealing, he spent most of his adult life broke. Nonetheless he had enough charm and style to always seem sharp and if not prosperous at least not depressed by his lack of funds, even if only in the generosity of the sharing of his talents and enthusiastic schemes, usually involving "the ponies," as we affectionately referred to horse racing, the only sport I remember the men of our clan being interested in back then.

My Uncle Lydie represented one extreme of the Irish-American philosophy as I learned it from these men. My father represented the other extreme, exemplified by these lines I wrote in a poem as a young man trying to explain him to myself: "My father usta say three things: Work, work/work."

My Uncle Lydie was famous for his lovely tenor voice, for remembering all the lyrics in the old tunes, for being willing to sing them at the drop of a hat or the opening of a bottle, and for losing everything again and again and not seeming to care. He won a contest once, singing on the radio during the Depression, and instead of doing something practical, he rented a tavern in nearby Union and threw a huge party with plenty of beer and booze and several large hams and loaves of bread and a spread like you never did see as I heard every time we passed the place.

He was good looking too, like all my uncles seemed to be when I was a boy, and seem still in my memory, in that kind of 1920s, hair combed back flat and smooth, clean-shaven style. And in the 1940s, when I was a boy, it seemed they were always in suits as well. Maybe because I remember them most from weddings and funerals and the occasional party for no reason at all. Usually at a certain point in the proceedings, when the noise level had increased from the growing excitement of adults getting high on drink and happy to be together again, someone would call for a song from my Uncle Lydie, and he would always oblige.

The song "Galway Bay," one of many sentimental Irish tunes Bing Crosby recorded, would bring tears to people's eyes when my Uncle Lydie sang it at parties, especially the line about how "The strangers came and tried to teach us their ways," which made me sad even before I understood that "the strangers" meant the English, who tried to impose their culture on the Irish for centuries. They were pretty successful at it too, on the surface. As I grew up I learned how the Irish language almost died, and for most of the country might as well be dead, despite the revival and occasional usage in public forums. Some aspects of the way the Irish once dressed, like kilts on men, disappeared entirely, after being outlawed for generations by the English "Penal Laws."

At one time the English were so intent on wiping out all vestiges of nationalism among the Irish, they outlawed what they considered to be the Irish "rebel" way the men combed their hair straight back with no part, à la Samuel Beckett—or my uncles. But I'm sure they were completely unaware of most of that, and they acted as if they didn't care, except when a song like "Galway Bay" produced a tear. I remember they used to pass around a letter from "the old country" which one of them would read out loud while they all chuckled and laughed at the backward country speech and ways of the West of Ireland peasants, which their parents had been. At the time I thought the letter was a kind of fiction, a mock letter from some imaginary Irishman in the old country, but now realize it was probably a real one.

At any rate, they would always get the biggest laugh when they'd read the part about the old I.R.A. soldier still fighting a battle from the 1920s. It was a kind of gag among them, the lost cause of the "republicans" to unite the Northern Counties with

176

the rest of free Ireland. And maybe in the 1940s and early '50s, when things were relatively quiet over there, it did seem like a joke to them. Or maybe the laughter was just a cover for the humiliation they had to endure when they were younger and there were signs and ads that read like the one my father carried in his wallet as a constant reminder of the way things had been not too many years before—"Irish Catholics Need Not Apply"—or maybe it was just embarrassment for the people they came from and their primitive arguments and ways of resolving them. Or maybe ... who knows. The main thing is, they laughed a lot back then and that was a lesson in itself. It seemed any and every catastrophe that befell our extended family could be turned into a joke and it was always one of my uncles to do it.

My aunts had their own ways of livening up any social gathering. Like my Aunt Peggy, Uncle Lydie's wife. They lived down the street with their two daughters and my Irish grandparents. Like all my aunts, I found her beautiful and fun. She would play the piano at any opportunity. I was impressed with her verve and lack of self-consciousness, since she often hit wrong notes and didn't seem to mind, nor did anyone else. She played loud barroom-style heavy chords with both hands ranging all over the keys, laughing and smiling and singing and obviously drunk, though that never occurred to me until later.

And my Aunt Mary, who lived next door with my Uncle John and their two sons and two daughters. She was the only Protestant in the family, though still of Irish descent. I hung out a lot in their house, appreciating her honest assessments of other family members and their follies. She seemed to be the most honest person I knew back then, when that was the most important trait I valued in anyone, including myself. But unlike my childish attempts at the truth, her adult bluntness always had a twist of humor in it to get a laugh even from me who felt self-conscious around them all, especially my uncles. Their eyes, though merry and full of life and some mysterious knowledge as well, had a glint of mockery to them. They were always making fun of something, including me, who always took myself too seriously, or perhaps the word is earnestly, because my heart was usually overflowing with excitement and gratitude at being alive and a part of this family and their world.

My "next door Uncle" John was a gentle man. He met Aunt Mary when she was his nurse at a TB sanitarium. Whenever he saw me he'd make some joke at my expense like all the other men in the family, only his jokes always seemed less critical and more understanding, as if he knew how vulnerable I felt around them. I'd always ask him to sing a song he once sang to me, and I could never get enough of, although it made no sense. It was the fun of seeing and hearing this lovely man sing something so childish and silly as: "Mairzy Doats'n' dozey dotes 'n' liddelamzy divey, akittalee divey too, wooden shoe." Which was a lot like the original Irish scat singing, called "lilting," that my Uncle Lydie also did so well. I only understood years later the words: "Mares eat oats, and does eat oats, and little lambs eat ivy. A kid'll eat ivy too. Wouldn't you?"

It seemed like I got him to sing that song to me every time he saw me by myself, as if he knew my joy and liked to see it crackle under my shy self-centered wonder at it all and the born with it desire to somehow never forget it, capture it in some form forever. At first I thought I'd do that with music, pestering my parents to let me take music lessons at three until they finally let me at four, so I could catch up to my five older musician siblings. The sixth, having passed away as a child before I was born, left a gap between me—the surprise—and the rest of them, so I felt like I had to work even harder to belong.

It wasn't long before I was playing everything they had in sheet music in the piano stool, from classical piano exercises to "It's the Same Old Shillelagh Me Father Brought from Ireland." My father couldn't play an instrument, but he sang often, usually the tin pan alley songs of his youth, and he would always ask me to play the piano for him on the rare occasions when he got home from work before we were already in bed. Some nights he'd whistle outside the house to wake us up if we were already asleep, it was a little ditty that he'd sing on other occasions, which we knew meant "I scream, you scream, we all scream for ice cream." My mother could never figure out how we always knew, as we'd run down the stairs to meet him just as he entered through the front door. She'd accuse him of spoiling us, which for a few years after WWII, it seemed like he did. And then that, like everything else, changed.

But back when I was still a little boy, it was my uncles that determined my life's direction and they didn't even know it, as I created secret scenarios for them and their mythlike stature in my own folklore. Like my uncle John, who in my mind, besides being

178

the gentlest man among my father and his brothers, was also in a way the most worldly. His subscription to *Esquire* magazine, which I would glance at when I could, seemed daring compared to my puritanical father's wariness of any reading beyond the daily papers, the *Racing Form*, and a few books by Catholic authors. And Uncle John had a job in the outside world working for the Prudential Life Insurance Company that he took the bus every morning to an office in Newark for, unlike my father and Uncle Lydie who worked either in my father's little hardware store or later in his little "home maintenance" business.

"The Pru" was the insurance company used by most of the neighborhood, and the insurance agent came around every month to pick up the premium payments personally. He was a short Jewish man who I got the idea my mother kind of liked because he flattered her and would hang around for hours in endless conversations with her. Though that wasn't that unusual. After my father left for work in the morning, the milkman, Mister McKenna, would stop with our bottles of milk and stand in the kitchen talking to my mother all through our breakfast, and he was an old white-haired Irishman, accent and all.

And if my father got home early enough, my uncle John would come over during our dinner, his family ate theirs earlier, and stand in our tiny kitchen, leaning against a sideboard drinking his bottles of beer and talking about politics and business and world events with my father while he ate, and the rest of us listened. I remember one conversation about how the Jews took care of their own, helping each other with their businesses so they could all make it up the ladder—my father sad and angry that the Irish, or at least the ones he knew, didn't do the same. I don't know if it was the same conversation, but I remember learning how my father had hired his father and one of his brothers to work for him once, and they ended up shortchanging the cash register and making jokes about it, as if my father were the fool for trying so hard to make it.

I felt sorry back then for the way my father had been treated and loved him for the fact he still helped his father and brother out, as well as a lot of other people in the family and the neighborhood. But he wasn't all kindness and forgiveness, with his judgments and fears, nor all business and work either, with his love of "the ponies," which included "making book" as they called taking bets, and his love of nice clothes—during his most prosperous

179

post-war years it seemed he always had a new hat and new shoes and a camel's-hair overcoat whose sensuous softness I remember coveting—and his drinking, though not long after I was born he gave that up.

My mother and aunts obviously found all these men entrancing in their laid-back Irish-American confidence man ways, as I did too, and I found my mother and aunts all beautiful and seemingly confident too, even though they all, men and women alike, seemed to lose that confidence if not their glow outside our extended family and neighborhood in the America they and the other neighborhood ethnics were a little afraid to take on, despite the fact that in the 1920s and '30s when they were coming of age, and on into the early '40s when I was a baby, the Irish were the dominant immigrant-underclass-on-the-rise in the USA no matter how many "Irish Catholics Need Not Apply" notices there were.

After all, F. Scott Fitzgerald's fiction defined the age to itself, and Jack Dempsey, who shared my mother's last name and we often speculated might be distantly related, conquered the world as heavyweight champion, and Jimmy Cagney's little Irish mug character took on the world of the movies, with nothing but guts and imagination, and won. And Bing Crosby was the American singing sensation whose mellow tones caused females to swoon as he brought the Irish anti-style of effortlessness, or so-natural-it-needs-no-cultivating, or just plain I'm-not-even-trying-to-impress-you-even-though-you-are-impressed technique to popular music, as well as movie acting.

"Bing" epitomized what was deliriously graceful about not seeming to try, something the Irish I grew up around seemed to personify, no matter what else they might pretend to be doing. My father and uncles made fun of my rummied-up Irish grandfather and his disdain for American values of hard work and upward mobility, while they fought their own battles, between and inside each other, over whether or not to pay homage to those American ideals—especially my father who was the most successful at it—or give in in the end to the fact they were mostly a bunch of grammar school dropouts whose unspoken ideal seemed to mirror their father's and what seemed to our unschooled eyes to be Bing's—to work as little as possible while having as many kids as you could.

My father's father was the only grandfather I had left. When he wasn't on his porch in his rocking chair, or up in his room, drinking, he'd sometimes venture across the street to the A&P for some booze, or in hard times, wander into the high school playing field at the bottom of our street to pick dandelions to make some horrible bathtub booze out of. Sometimes he'd forget to put his pants on and make a laughingstock of himself bending over the grass in his underwear.

He was the neighborhood character, the joke, the local unshaven drunk, difficult to understand on the rare occasions when he spoke, because of the booze and his Irish accent. And yet to us he was "Himself," the patriarch of our clan that filled so many houses on our one-and-a-half-block street that taxi drivers and bus drivers used to refer to it as "Lally's alley." No matter what "the Americans" thought of my grandfather, I was brought up to show nothing but respect for him, and in fact, I did respect him. He seemed mysterious and powerful, because no matter how much my father and uncles made fun of him behind his back, their voices still betrayed a deep awe and even fear, though I interpreted it as a kind of honor, toward their drunken hardened old man.

My mother would say every few days, "Did you visit your grandfather this week?" and if I'd shake my head no, she'd send me down to see him. If he wasn't on the porch drinking, my grandmother would send me up to their room, where I'd enter kind of shyly, and he'd ask, "Who are you?" and I'd say, "Michael," and when I saw that meant nothing I'd add, "Jimmy's youngest," and he'd say, "Pass me me bottle," and that would be that. I'd stay for a while in silence and then quietly make my exit when he was looking out the window with a faraway look in his eyes. Sometimes I'd run into "Pop Lally," as we kids called him, in the A&P buying his booze in his old soiled hat and his unshaven face, just a rummy to the manager and others keeping a wary eye on him, but still my grandfather to me, and he wouldn't recognize me—or maybe he was just sparing me the embarrassment of his presence in their world, the Americans he had deep scorn for in all their chasing after money and possessions.

Those principles my grandfather seemed to stand for, of working as little as possible while having as many kids as you could, seemed to be embodied by Bing Crosby, the paragon of Irish virtue and success when I was a boy, because he seemed to never work too hard and certainly had a lot of kids, which I now realize had a lot to do with his popularity in the outside world as well, and was kind of true, in that he kept his efforts to himself, even though he obviously worked very hard at his "career," and despite the fact that some of his kids weren't too happy with the kind of father he was, accusing him later of a mean and arbitrary discipline that went against his easygoing image. My father and his siblings wouldn't have been surprised by that. I remember him telling me how when he was a boy, his father would line up all his kids at the end of the week and walk down the line slapping each of them saying, "That's for whatever I didn't catch you at this week."

But no matter what kind of father Bing Crosby was, or how much effort he really put into his "art," it seemed to people like my family, that with the obvious ease of his talent, he got paid for just being himself, and wouldn't that be a nice thing to have happen to you, which I was sure would happen to me, as sure as I knew I was a genius before a teacher told my family I was and they responded with a kind of denial that said you should live with him before you draw any conclusions like that. Like my father, even though he too was guilty if it, I could never understand that kind of refusal to support your own, that I found too common among the Irish-Americans I grew up around, and later saw among the Irish in the old country as well. I used to summarize it with a saying I never really heard this way, but in different words heard constantly: "You're a good-looking boy; who do you think you are?" It was what the Irish called "a backhanded compliment" and I hated them for it and it wasn't until years later that I realized I did it too, when my first wife pointed out to me that I never said anything nice and complimentary to her without immediately saying something to take it back, like "That's a beautiful dress, but where did you get those shoes?"

When, in an attempt to understand my own origins, I found myself studying the history of the Irish and their culture, I came to the conclusion that under the several centuries of England's most repressive rule, an Irishman who stood up for himself or stood out from his fellows would be singled out and made into a martyr. In other words, any Irish Catholic man who acted like he had a right to do and say whatever he pleased in his own country was cut down to size in some way, either imprisoned, exiled, or executed as an example. And that became a frightening but real part of the culture, that the people themselves incorporated, a kind of humorous verbal cutting down to size of anyone who attempted to

182

stand above the crowd, as a kind of insurance, to save the best from punishment or death for too much pride.

Not that the Irish culture and people don't make heroes out of those martyrs, and legends out of their attributes and struggles, but they don't particularly want to see their own sons ending up that way. So when anyone seemed to be a little too full of themselves, their family and friends would make sure to knock that idea right out of them, with cutting humor, or fists if it came to that. So if you wanted to get ahead with these people, you had to maintain a sense of humor and humility about yourself that I just couldn't seem to master as a kid who knew he was smart, knew he was good-looking—weren't the ladies always telling me so?—and knew he intuited things that people kept secret or didn't know. In fact I was burning inside with the truth I thought I was born to tell, and there's nothing more dangerous among a people who have been kept in virtual bondage for centuries, than the honest unembellished flat-out not even humorously projected truth.

In the popular American culture of my youth, Bing Crosby was the embodiment of that more common Irish cultural attitude, a man whose voice was like silk and whose good looks, even though he was losing his hair and his ears stuck out, helped make him not only a singing star but a movie star. And yet he still depended partly for his popularity on never taking himself or his talent too seriously and often teamed up with an Englishman—Bob Hope—who would see that he never did, by cutting him down to size with an acid wit that only seemed harmless because Hope was not as handsome or talented. But Hope's jokes could be caustic and would have been deadly if Bing didn't stand still for them so graciously and modestly and self-effacingly in that Irish way I couldn't help rebelling against.

But before I did, when I was still a boy struggling with my own version of the truth but unable to express it, I loved being among these people, in our neighborhood, still sometimes called "Cabbage Hill" or "Cabbage Town" from all the Irish immigrant families that crowded its streets. It was a relatively friendly neighborhood when I was a boy. Of course among the kids there were always fights of one kind or another, sometimes even ending in tragedy. And the grownups knew how to get into a brawl as well. But because our neighborhood was a part of the immigrant corridor that ran alongside the railroad tracks, and thus was not very big, we had to learn how to get along. Most of the neighborhood

Irish or Italians or "colored" or Jews, had moved up from Newark, which we called "downtown," where the ethnic neighborhoods were larger and more distinctly separate, and where the "race wars," as the newspapers then called fights between gangs of males from one ethnic group fighting another, were big and deadly. My mother's mother used to tell me stories of when she was a girl in Newark how during big fights between the Germans and the Irish, the men would come home to get their wives' carving and chopping knives.

My neighborhood seemed too small and too mixed to sustain any kind of true and lasting animosity. Although it often did. On our street lived an Italian family, with two brothers known informally as "Loaf" and "Half a Loaf," or more formally as "Loaf of Bread" and "Half a Loaf of Bread." They were sweet-natured guys as far as I could see and friends of my older brothers, as their mother was one of my mother's closest friends.

But once the brothers were drinking in a local bar when one of my brothers came in with his Irish-American father-in-law, both of them cops at the time, and an altercation started between my brother's father-in-law and an Italian-American and naturally my brother had to take his father-in-law's side, and naturally "Loaf" and "Half a Loaf" had to take the Italian's side. When the owner called the cops because the brawl was getting out of hand, one of the cops who showed up was one of my brothers-in-law who naturally helped my brother and his father-in-law win the fight before arresting the "Italians," including the brothers from across the street famous for their bread-related nicknames. Their mother never talked to my mother again. I remember my mother crying in the kitchen and my asking her what was the matter and her telling me she missed talking to Missus Iantasco.

But the clashes were minimal and not as deadly as they were in Newark where we all had family that still lived in the old neighborhoods. And despite all our differences, it seemed like we all belonged to the same world, compared to those who lived outside our neighborhood. The further you got from the few blocks near the railroad tracks, the more assimilated you became. I knew Irish-Americans who thought that by moving two blocks further from the tracks, they were free of any possibility of their daughters getting mixed up with Italians, or vice versa, depending on the ethnicity of the family moving.

It seemed like the people who lived in those more "American" neighborhoods were the real strangers and foreigners to us, even some of our distant uncles and aunts and cousins, who always seemed to be smirking a little at our more shanty ways when they were around. But behind the closed doors of our homes, we were wary of the ethnic "others" in the neighborhood, and as I grew older and spent more time in the homes of these other ethnic groups, I discovered how true that was for them too.

For instance we thought of Italians we weren't close to as what would be described, if complimentary, as "earthy" but came out more in private as "animalistic," meaning they seemed meaner in physical confrontations and spoiled their sons and used a lot of oil in their food and hair. And of course the Jews, meaning again the ones who weren't in our circle of friends, were seen as better at business and helping each other make money, or in less positive terms, as cheap and only interested in money and their own kind, who we sarcastically called "the chosen people." And of course, the Slavic-Americans were even more thickheaded and more worthy of carrying bricks than the Irish. When one of my sisters married the son of Polish immigrants, my father was fond of remarking that before he married into our family he had never set foot in a restaurant or on a train, as though we were the upper class of this working-class neighborhood, which my father and others thought we were.

Recently I ran into an Italian-American friend from Jersey who complained to me of his ex-wife's Irish-American family being "coldhearted," saying, "Hey, you're Irish, you know how vindictive they can be. I mean, Italians, we yell and say we're gonna kill each other, but a couple of days later we're hugging and kissing. The fucking Irish don't ever forget." I didn't mention my mother's Italian best friend from across the street who never spoke to her again, in fact I joined him in that kind of understanding laughter people who have shared a common past and moved a great distance from it know. But it still made me bristle inside thinking, hey, the Irish are sentimental sweethearts compared to some of the frighteningly menacing Italians I encountered as a kid, except of course for "The Loafs" and all the other exceptions.

As I grew up I became estranged from the Irish-Americans because of their narrow-mindedness—their petty prejudices and fears of other groups—especially of the people they called "colored" in the 1950s of my teenage years. They considered the

185

"colored"—at least those who weren't friends of the family—unambitious, or "lazy," and deviantly, sinfully, even mysteriously, sexual. As though we didn't share some traits in common. In fact, I couldn't help noticing that among all the ethnic groups around us, we Irish seemed to have most in common with the "colored," from partying at the drop of a hat, to having large families and often ending up with an abandoned appliance on the porch, or an aging Cadillac in mid-repair in the driveway or street.

As I got to know these various ethnic groups better, I found they had the same stereotypical ideas about other groups as we had about them. I also found that despite the usual objections against stereotyping, they all seemed to be proud of the very traits used to stereotype them. Especially when they popped up at the movies, which were not so much an escape as a reinforcement of our secret hopes and fears. One of life's greatest thrills for me was waiting for the show to begin, when suddenly the lights began to dim. I often felt like crying in gratitude for what movies did for my heart as I fell in love with the women and men and children I found in them—like the Irish-American child actress Margaret O'Brien.

I felt the movies talked right to me in my seat in the dark, in love with the world in my heart, and in awe of the ways that were sometimes portrayed in the art of the silver screen and its stars. My sisters were usually forced to take me to the movies with them on Sunday afternoons, after what we called "the big dinner," when my father'd take a nap and us youngest kids were sent out to the movies. It was actually a great time in films for people like we were then, Irish-Catholic-Americans, devout in our faith and the old Latin rituals, happy to be a part of America's post-war prosperity and peace, no matter how minimal or illusional. I remember the warmth and gladness *Going My Way* with Bing Crosby and Barry Fitzgerald created in my family, even though I was only three when it won a ton of Oscars—it was as if the awards were going to the Irish in us.

I loved even more that movie's sequel, *The Bells of St. Mary's,* with Bing the same "Father O'Malley," which sounded like Lally, and Ingrid Bergman as the most beautiful nun in the world. I saw myself and my brothers and cousins in those films, among those tough little city boys who still respected "the Father" and all those old Irish-Catholic movie clichés forever connected to Bing Crosby and his "Father O'Malley" and Ingrid Bergman's nun who

186

became real a few years later in first grade at Our Lady of Sorrows Grammar School where I was taught by Sister Gemma, one of the kindest most gentle women I ever encountered.

But by second grade, when I was ready for my first real date, it was the end of the 1940s and of the era when the Irish were the dominant immigrant group sentimentalized in popular culture. The obvious contender for new champ of American popular ethnicity was Italian-Americans, with the ascendancy in the '40s of Frank Sinatra as the successor to Bing, and the soon to follow Italian-American crooners, Perry Como, Tony Martin, Dean Martin, Tony Bennett, *et al.*

In the movies, Italian neo-realism was having its influence, and in sports there was DiMaggio and the original championship Rockys—Marciano and Graziano. Joe Louis, "The Brown Bomber," an earlier African-American heavyweight champion, brought pride and a new awareness to the people then formally known as "Negro," and his popularity, along with Nat King Cole's—even when his TV show couldn't find sponsors to keep it on the air for fear of losing consumers among Southern whites—foreshadowed the eventual cultural rise and influence of African-Americans.

The music that seemed to bind our clan together was fading too, except for wakes and weddings, as my two oldest brothers, after stints in the service at the end of World War II, left for different Catholic colleges on the G.I. Bill, one of them marrying an Italian-American, the other becoming a priest. The third was drafted during the Korean War after which my father's business went downhill, which he blamed on the Republicans, saying, "Count the number of stores for lease and if there's more than a few, you know there's a Republican in the White House." And the problems of growing up a boy in the New Jersey of the 1950s seemed overwhelming to me.

So I did what so many Irish men in previous generations had done, including my namesake grandfather, by joining the "wild geese" in a flight out of the ethnic homelands and into the foreign cultures of other lands, or at least other neighborhoods, or at least other ethnic groups inside our neighborhood as I went on my first formal date, in second grade, a few months before I turned nine. I asked the prettiest Italian girl in the class to go to the movies with me to see *Quo Vadis*, an appropriately Roman epic spectacle.

Not too many years later, entering my teens, what looked like monster-sized meaty Italians, in long black cars with dark

187

windows you couldn't see into, warned me away from another Italian beauty from the neighborhood, and I moved even further away in ethnic loyalty though only a few more blocks, to ask out an African-American girl, which for a while severed my ties not only to my family and the Irish of my neighborhood, but to their image of what I might be or become, and freed me to leave the neighborhood far behind not long after.

I did it by joining the service, and before all the courts-martial and civilian troubles, the jobs playing jazz and R&B in segregated shacks in the South and "black" fiancées, I received the only piece of writing I ever got from my father. It was a St. Patrick's Day card on which he had written in his seventh-grade-dropout scrawl: "to the only other Irishman in the family" and I remember feeling a burst of pride as well as a connection to the past I was only beginning to fathom.

Many years later, just after my father died, on my first trip outside the States, I was standing on a corner in Old San Juan, Puerto Rico, thinking about how other cultures had spread their influence around the world in practical ways you could see and hear and taste, like the Chinese restaurant nearby, or the Italian one I'd eaten in the night before, or the Indian shop owners in the store I'd just left, or the African influence in the music and style of the people passing by. I wondered what the Irish had contributed to this worldly mix of cultural influences—this was before I understood how much the Irish had contributed to American popular music, from Country & Western to rock'n'roll, I was only aware then of how much African-Americans had contributed to all that—when suddenly among the people passing I noticed a boy, about ten, talking Spanish to his friends, typically Puerto Rican in his style, obviously a native of the island, but with red hair and freckles and a twinkle in his eyes that reminded me of my uncles, and I thought, Ah, that's what the Irish have spread throughout the world—themselves. And I was happy to be one of them.

188

VOTE FOR ME

I've always loved politics. Well, almost always. In 1948, when I was six I picked Truman over Dewey and felt great when I was proven right despite what the adults and papers predicted.

Later, in the early '50s when my father went to work for the Essex County, New Jersey, Democratic machine, I learned why old-time politics worked so well. With my sisters and brothers I put hundreds of flyers under windshield wipers in church parking lots on Sunday mornings, or called shut-ins and old folks and invalids and offered them rides to the polls, my older siblings driving but me providing the reassuring voice on the phone to these people all alone in the world except for the Democratic Party.

I attended rallies and whistlestops at the local train station. I argued with my schoolmates who wore "I Like Ike" buttons or put down Adlai Stevenson for being an "egghead." I knew how that felt, when in the early grades, before I turned more thuggish, my high marks and obvious brains seemed like an insult to the tougher kids. But that's not how the big boys won elections.

My father showed me how, when neighborhood Italians or Irish or blacks needed something done, like one time when Mrs. Magliari's son was off in Europe in the Army and his grandmother died. The Army didn't give leave for any family death except a parent, so my father called the Congressman the machine had gotten elected and told his secretary what needed to be done and within hours Mrs. Magliari's son was on a plane heading home. Next election day she called my dad to ask who she and the other twenty-one Magliaris should vote for.

I remember my father being home on election nights, a rarity since he always seemed to be out working by the time I went to bed. But on those nights he'd let me stay up and watch the returns on primitive TVs in black-and-white and give a running commentary, which educated me in the ways of those days as he would call each vote within a tiny margin. He knew his people.

He avoided the election night parties because by then he'd given up drinking and he'd always been a kind of shrinking violet anyway. But when he had to go, he'd take one of my brothers and a brother-in-law, both cops at the time, in their off-duty gear but still packing their civilian guns to act as bodyguards because the Democratic Party in that part of Jersey could get very rough when people disagreed among themselves.

I remember watching the 1956 Democratic Convention with my dad, and him predicting that JFK, a new young senator making a nomination speech, might be president some day. My father said, "His father has enough money to make it happen."

I saw Bobby Kennedy at the upstate New York basketball Catholic college I went to for a few months before I got kicked out. He was campaigning for his brother Jack and had us all on his side as he described what he planned to do to the Teamsters and mobsters when his brother got in. Well, we know who did who in.

We watched the Nixon-Kennedy debates on a communal TV in an aging dorm in Olean, New York, where the Depression had yet to end, and grinned as we accepted that our boy would win. I was on the Jersey State Parkway when he died, on my way back to the barracks at Fort Monmouth when I saw cars pull off the road, their drivers sobbing. As I slowed to pay the toll, the guy who took my quarter told me, "He's been shot, the president."

I got back in time to hear a name the black guys worried for a moment might mean them and were relieved when it turned out to be a white guy after all. We watched it in the barracks rec room which consisted of a TV, some chairs and ashtrays and us standing around the black-and-white as Oswald got it live.

By the time LBJ got officially elected, I was married and stationed in Spokane, where me and my wife listened to his acceptance speech on the radio of the two-tone '56 Pontiac I bought as a sign of my newfound married stability. I almost cried when that big Texas lug drawled out the words "We Shall Overcome" as though he meant it, and for a minute thought maybe some things might change.

But when I got a call in the middle of an August night a year

190

later to chart weather maps for bombers carrying the big one toward mainland China and found out the next day about Tonkin Bay, I took a resolute left turn in my political direction. So that by '68 I found myself in Iowa running for sheriff on the Peace and Freedom ticket, and getting thrown out of the national convention when Eldridge Cleaver didn't dig my choice for his running mate—a wise and tough old hillbilly woman named Peggy Terry.

He opted for the Yippie clown Jerry Rubin, and when I tried to argue Cleaver down several big Black Panthers picked me up and physically threw me out of the caucus room. What a shame, imagine what a stir the combination of an urban black ex-con running with a coalminer's wife from the white trash South would have made, and the questions they might have raised.

I had my doubts by then about my fellow lefties as I saw some of them gloat when RFK went down. By '72 I had turned myself so inside out I was living in a feminist collective in DC and driving to Miami to protest the Republican Convention's Nixon bash in gender-bending, mind-fucking demonstrations that left me shaken and wondering what was more absurd, the Republicans doing their best to create some hate to motivate support for phonies and sociopaths or me and my friends in various stages of outrageous doped-up drag in support of something supposedly more humane and caring. It was daring, but debilitating and I left any idea of changing things behind.

By '76 I didn't care anymore which side was whose and Gerald Ford looked like a nice guy. But Carter got me with his aw shucks Southern anti-charm until I couldn't help but root for him when he got in and started saying things long overdue. But people didn't want to know that it was time to go slow and maybe clean up the wreckage of our collective past.

As he brought peace to the Middle East, or part of it, and championed human rights in places where there'd been none, I saw it coming, I knew they wouldn't run when he dismissed the bad actors from the CIA and military. And sure enough their fingerprints were all over the Iran deal, when Iran took our hostages they wouldn't let go until Ronnie was elected. Does anybody remember what *his* followers were braying? "It's a new morning in America."

Unfortunately, what we woke up to was twelve years of all we loved about this country steadily decaying. So when Clinton came along it was good to see people make a choice for something more

191

progressive once again. And then it began, as peace came to more of the Middle East and human rights regained importance in the political arena, the right wing decided to get rough and with the help of Christian ayatollahs put out propaganda often worse than just old-fashioned lies.

Did anyone notice in the first reports on that guy who shot up the White House, he had a bumper sticker on his truck that said "Rush Is Right"? Does anybody else fantasize having their own radio show to let people know there's an answer to the hypocrites who preach family values as they marry for the third time and hide behind labels that don't apply, like conservative champion of the middle class.

As we used to say in the old leftist days: There's only two classes. Those who run the show—they used to call them the ruling class because they ruled in the decisions that affected the rest of our lives—and the working class, because we did the work while they made the decisions. If the ruling class rules and the working class works, what would the middle class do? Middle?

Oh I know, I know, that's all old hat. And it's more complicated than that. But I still think some good old-fashioned radicalism could save the day. Like, let's eliminate the CIA, the NSA, and the DEA and give the billions saved to the NEA. And while we're at it, let's eliminate all secret agencies and budget items and get back to the old Constitution, where nothing goes on that isn't out in the open if it concerns our democracy and the people we vote for to serve it.

So hey, vote for me and I'll see what I can do.

Irish Oppression Poem

Look at it on a map.
It's an island.
How can there be a "North"
and a "South" that see
themselves as two different
lands. There's only the one
land, an island, Ireland.
Yeah, it's had other names,
still does, but you know
the place I mean, where
the "wearin' of the green"
doesn't mean as much as
here. What matters there
is a job. It was always a poor
island, not like England,
big and in sight of a
continent. No, out at
the edge of that world,
all alone, small and
insular, like the other
places we think of when
we think of islands.
Only this is an island
of white people. Conquered
and oppressed for centuries
by other white people.
Kept poor and exploited

and all the clichés so
many nowadays think only
apply to people of color.
Like having your culture
deliberately destroyed,
your language and your
way of dress. How many
here have ever even heard
a word of Gaelic, how
many there would ever had
if the patriots had not
secured at least the
Southern counties' freedom.
Not many speak it as their
mother tongue anymore,
a handful here and there
in the West where it's
so barren the English
didn't have as much to
damage in their thousand
year British Reich. That
sounds too harsh, but how
about this? Did you know
that Irishmen wore kilts
just like the Scots once?
Of course you don't because
the English created the
Penal Codes that said anyone
who practiced their religion
or spoke their language or
wore their customary clothes
or even combed their hair
straight back without a part,
like Beckett later did, would
be thrown in jail or sent on
a prison ship to early America
there to work off years of
servitude with few more rights
than African slaves or sent
to Australia and the penal
colonies there so far away

from loved ones, families,
mates and kids and home, or
killed outright, or
let starve to death.
Cromwell made the Irish
rivers run red with the
blood of women and children
whose bloated bodies clogged
the rivers' bends and could
be seen by journalists of
the day who described the
devastation in a way that
made it clear they had never
seen worse even in the then
cursed oppression of India
or Africa, and later in
the last century when all
means of subsistence had been
stripped from the natives of
this land, so completely that
a man could not own more than
a pig and if he did a Brit
could buy it off him for that
value, and all they had to
feed their kids was the
American Indian potato,
and when that went they
did too. It's called a
famine still, as if the words
we use now like genocide and
holocaust do not apply, as if
the wealthy English and their
proxy landlords didn't eat as
well as always in those years,
as if the drawings before
cameras of kids all eyes and
bloated bellies don't match
any seen more recently in
Somalia and the Sudan, as if
there weren't accounts of
twenty people living in a

piece of mud and twigs with
all the grass stains on their
lips from eating all there was
until the rats come out to
gnaw to death the ones still
living, as if half the popula-
tion didn't disappear in only
a few years, and never recover.
There's fewer people on the
entire island than on the
island of Manhattan, and most
of them are in the North,
where it's still going on.
Where up until the 1960s,
if you were Catholic you
had no representation, no
voice in the government that
ruled your every move, you
had no chance for anything
but the lowest jobs in your
own country, where slights
and inconveniences could
lead to prison or death
still, just like in the
old days because it's still
the old days there. Where
English soldiers shove the
muzzles of their guns through
the window of your car and
into your chest until they
find out you're an American
and then begin to treat you
with just a touch more respect.
Hey, I'm as tired as you of
all the victimization contests
we've all been subjected to.
Others have had it as bad or
maybe worse. But the curse
of this land is that it began
over a thousand years ago
and is still going on with

the same oppressor doing
its best to represent itself
as on the victim side of the
line. I take no pride in
IRA bombs that mutilate and
murder innocent people, or
even guilty ones. I wish
they'd stop. But how else
get the world's attention.
It's a mess the English made,
and like good boys and girls
they should be made to clean
it up themselves. Give back
the land to those who live
there, even the descendants
of the Protestants they sent
to displace the natives, it's
been too many centuries to
give or take that back, but
give the Irish Ireland or
there will always be those
who will fight to take it
back. There is so much more.

What's Goin' On

I'm too wiped out to write a poem today—I can hardly breathe—
the trees I love so much look gray instead of green and they can't
even be seen from two blocks away—they're crying, with the rest
of the universe—because they know it's only gonna get worse
unless we stop pretending we're so numb or dumb or powerless to
change, and it's all the same anyway, the power's there, we can see
it in the way each tree expresses its own destiny despite all we've
done to end their role as givers of the air we breathe—can you
conceive a day when all the trees will be as gray as some of us—I
can, if we don't dust off all our concepts of what power means—it
isn't in our brains or in our muscles or even in our genes, though
that is where it might have been—it's in the ways we look at who
we are and how we use the power that's there—and like Selby
says, if we plug a lamp in a socket we get light, if we plug a fork in
we get a lesson in the misuse of power—we have the power to elect
our leaders—if we misuse it because we don't want to hear bad
news, or views that contradict our wish to keep on consuming as if
there is no end in sight—we might end up with leaders who stick
forks into the universe getting us fried instead of shedding some
light on this darkest of nights in our human history—and I don't
mean to say we haven't done some things right—we know we
have, but that's all in the past and now we've got some more
important things to do—I wish I knew what they were so I could
tell them to you—but I'm trying to understand what the need is
too—It's like the way I used to be with women—that feeling of
needing them to solve my problems of guilt and sin once and for
all was a tall order for anyone, let alone some stranger in a

198

strangely familiar intimacy where the air we breathed seemed heavy not because of the poisons we put there but because it was the same air that clung to the contours of our bodies when we tried to make them fit and filled our lungs when we sucked each other's lungs empty—damn, this is starting to sound like a bad romance novel—see how quickly it gets away—when what I was trying to say was there's got to be a connection between the way we treat each other in our most intimate relations and the ways we treat the trees and what's going on is this I miss you so fucking much sometimes all I can think of is your smile—there's a bird outside my window with a red head and wings and a yellow butterfly that all reminds me of Spring back East when I was growing up, only then the air I saw them through was invisible, but this air I can see, it's making the green of the nearby trees seem more gray today, and the ones only a little farther way, I can't even make out, let alone the nearby once majestic mountains that are now just more contours lost in the haze as they call it on better days, or smog like they're saying today, but it's still a cliché for poison— what poisoned the beauty that made us so awestruck in each other's presence, unable to wait to touch and kiss and see if we fit, that made us laugh with delight like the kids we all are because the initial fright that this might be one night, and that's all, turns out to be only a kid's projection, I mean we got happy just being in each other's direction, like when we were kids and it was Spring and even in LA the days got more fruitful and rich with the promise we saw in each other's eyes, but somehow that promise dies when we neglect to nurture and protect it, just like the air and the sky and the sea and the trees and all the living energy that is the universe we seem to be rejecting—we neglected our godgiven rights and responsibilities, and the whole place is dying, damn, I'm trying to come up with a way we can get back the love again, the way I love these trees and can feel that they're crying like I want to cry—I'm afraid I'm gonna start crying and never stop— I'm afraid I'll never cry—

The Healing Poem

When I first wrote this poem
    I believed there was a healing going on—
        a profound healing. I thought it was
no accident that movies like
    Field of Dreams and *Rain Man*
        (no matter how we might feel about
their politics or art) were proving
    the lie in all the cynical projections
        of what people want. What they want
is a healing to take place.

    Gorbachev became a hero
        around the world not because
he knew how to manipulate
    the media—remember his speeches?
        It wasn't *him,* it was what he represented,
the healing of a wound almost
    a century old. Wasn't it obvious
        by the response of the world to him,
or to the Chinese students in
    Tienanmen Square, or the release
        of Nelson Mandela, or the fall of the
Berlin Wall, or the Russian people
    standing up to the tanks & the old ideas—
        it was a healing we all wanted?

& hey, I knew all about "wilding"

and gang rape and gang violence
and gang stupidity and cowardice
and all the rest. I was in a couple
of gangs when I was a kid. I also
know the cops can be a gang too sometimes.
I come from a family of cops, &
if you don't think it's tough being
stopped by the police & hearing
"What's your brother gonna say?"
—just think about a cop asking—
"What's this gonna do to Ma?"

But I think we know and so do
those kids what's good for the soul,
the spirit, the heart. Yet when that good
has been torn apart by public figures
who act as if they have no responsibility
toward this world—whose world is it anyway?
Or rock'n'rollers or movie stars
or TV celebrities who speak out
about pollution and then personalize it in
their own lives by polluting hearts
and souls and minds with messages
they take no responsibility for.

And I'm not talking about sexual
jokes and innuendoes. I'm talking
about violence that is presented as power
and reward and even inspirational.
I'm talking about accepting and even
celebrating the cynical attitudes that everyone
seemed to acquiesce to in the '80s—
the "Reagan Years"—for which we are
all now paying the price. I'm talking about
adding to the confusion and fear
and hatred and rage by accepting
the unacceptable, by ignoring the unignorable,
by pretending reality is worse than
it is and then giving in to that pretension
until it becomes reality. I WANT THE HEALING.

And I believe with everything that's in me
          that even those who will write parodies,
                    or speak them, as soon as they finish reading this,
of what they can easily dismiss
          and turn into a self-defensive joke
                    about my own hypocrisy or pretensions—
even the wits who can turn misery
          into charisma, and though I know I'm
                    no wit I also know I sometimes can do it too—
even us poor victims of our own
          delusions of sincerity, no matter how hip,
                    WANT A HEALING TO OCCUR and want it now.

The whole world is longing and
          has been longing for just that.
                    Why else is Jesus so popular? Or Buddha?
Or the Mohammed of the real Koran?
          What is it that repulses us in the struggle
                    of the Arabs and the Jews, or Bosnians and
Serbs or Blacks and Whites in
          South Africa or here not so long ago,
                    but the lack of a healing between two cultures
that generate all our own fears
          about differences, and the rage
                    that fear of the different and unknown
can create in total strangers
          when they see us tearing down
                    the walls that make those differences.

I've said it before and I'm not
          gonna stop—I don't care if
                    you're from *Time* because you think
some "star" is reading poetry
          somewhere, or from the academy
                    because you think one of your own is there—
or look down your nose at those
          whose poetry is accessible and
                    even vital to people who don't care—
that's not what people come out to hear—
          I believe they come for the healing, for in
                    hearing the troubles and longings and truth

202

of other lives, no matter how famous or rich
or unknown or Jewish or young or frail or
perfect or a wreck, they see the common thread,
that it isn't about women and men
and young and old and black and white
and rich and poor and famous and unknown,
it's about this deep and abiding and
relentless yearning for a healing to
take place in all of us and between all of us.

It's not even about humans and animals
and nature and commerce and all that either.
Because even there, even businesses and trees
and cars and the very air and sea
and earth itself are making that
longing known. You can hear it in the wind
and smell it on the flower. All creation
is crying out for a healing to take place.
It is time. It is beyond time, it is timeless.
And yes of course it begins with me
and you, who else? And yes I have
felt it since we met and held each other in a way
that offered no defenses no obeisance
to the differences that we know so well
and so truly are just the flowering of the creative
imagination of the universe and not
a reason to run or quit or give up in
frustration and anger and cynicism. No,
the differences only help us to see
how much we are the same in our souls—
soulmates for sure. How else explain that two
such unlikely people can feel
so comfortable in each other's arms,
can ignore all the warnings from past experiences
and cynical friends that something
is unreal if there is no doubt, no struggle.
The only struggle is with acceptance—acceptance
of the truth. And the truth is
we all need a healing. And you
and I can feel it happening for us, in ways that
go beyond our simple male and

femaleness, our white and blackness,
   our age differences, our family and career and
neighborhood and all the other
  differences, beyond our humanness—
   a healing that like Selby says heals those issues
for all time, in all eternity, for all
  the years we've spent on earth so far
   and all we will continue to spend. And if that
can happen for us, in the simple act
  of *trust*—what more can it do for
   the rest of the world.

I never believed people who said
  you can't make movies or music or
   books that don't have violence or superficial values
or all the bullshit negativity
  this town and every town and
   every business tries to lay on those of us
who refuse to relinquish our
  innocence and hope because
   we have not succumbed to the dope of
giving up. Hey I know this sounds
  like preaching, so hold me accountable.
   I'm talking about a healing here, that I needed
desperately all my life and still do,
  and that I finally feel has truly begun
   with you. And not just you, but others too.
Oh people people let us start anew
  and pledge right now to each other
   that we will no longer take part in any project
whether business or art or any affair
  of the heart or collaboration or conversation
   or celebration or even thought that isn't true.
So let's start, right here, with me
  & you—& you & you & you & you
   & you...

DUES AND DON'TS

Did you dig the full moon out there tonight?
Sometimes when you see a sight as pure and
powerful as that, it makes you feel like
maybe everything is all right? Don't it?

I don't know why I love you like I do—
I don't even know if I do.
Hey, I'm not talking about you.
I'm just trying to get this poem off the ground
so I'll have an excuse to stick around
even if nothing else gets done.
You know what it's like to be white and male
and then fail? We got no excuse.
We're supposed to rule the world.
At least that's what others say when
they don't get their way—or they feel like
we might be in it—their way that is.
But when we don't get ours
we can't even get any sympathy.
Hey, I'm talking about me—
and the dues I've paid just being afraid
to be what you see—white and male and
over 21 and free. I just don't want to
lie anymore—or be lied to.
I believe we all deserve our due,
as they used to say, like due respect
and dignity, no matter what kind of

image we see when we
look at each other. I'm so
tired of the Turks and the Kurds
and the Croats and the Serbs and the
Armenians and the Azerbaijanis
and the Hutus and the Tutsis and the
Catholics and the Protestants
and the Jews and the Arabs and the
Koreans and the Blacks and the
Indians and the Pakistanis and the
New Yorkers and the bridge and tunnelers
and the Valley and the beaches
and the artists and the businessmen and
the criminals and the dope and the
politicians and the promises and the
poets and the truth and the secret police
and the propaganda and the spies and the
lies the lies the lies the fucking lies
that they tell to protect us from the
other guys' lies as if we might all die
if we realize that they ain't as
bad as we're supposed to believe or
as good as they want us to think they are
and neither are we and ain't it about time
we all stopped doing the "our kind" bit
and tried being the only kind that can
actually sit down and figure this shit out
without fighting if we try to approach
the truth with respect and acceptance
that we can only get closer never all
the way there but if we listen carefully
we might hear at least where it is so
we can at least know which way to go.

Did you dig the full moon out there tonight?
Sometimes when you see a sight as pure and
powerful as that, it makes you feel like
maybe everything *is* all right? Doesn't it?

GIMME SHELTER

Give me shelter from this sadness and confusion.
Give me shelter from this loneliness and feelings of despair.
Give me shelter from this fear of never finding a solution to this
    killing of each other—of the earth and of the air.
Give me shelter from hypocrisy and lies and hype and self-
    righteousness—my own or anyone else's.
Give me shelter from all judgments of who is right and who is
    wrong, or who is weak and who is strong or who is a
    failure and who is a success or who should wear the pants
    and who should wear the dress.
Give me shelter from my anger from my rage and violent fear.
Give me shelter from feeling like a helpless little baby when the
    one I think I love's not here.
Give me shelter from confusing love of God and love of women.
Give me shelter from the habit of flirtation even when I don't
    mean it and from the idea that I really always do.
Give me shelter from thinking only of myself when I'm
    pretending to be thinking only of you.
Give me shelter from all the bullshit games I played to try and
    make it in this town.
Give me shelter from all regrets, even over that time I wore a
    gown. Only kidding, I don't regret it at all. No, there I go
    again, sure I do, because it makes you think of something
    I can't control. I don't mean wearing gowns or dresses,
    once was enough, but what you think of someone who
    would do that.
Give me shelter from even caring who's got control.

Give me shelter from that whole idea.

Give me shelter from the feeling that the only shelter is when you are in my arms.

Give me shelter from believing that you won't like me unless I turn on the charm.

Give me shelter from mixing up God's gifts I was born with, or learned, with the recognition and rewards others have earned with theirs.

Give me shelter from all ideas that do not come from love.

Give me shelter from writing poems at the last minute before rushing to a reading and then getting up and expecting to come up with some sort of positive and heart-hitting resolution that dispels all our confusion and frustration and heals our hearts and war-torn psyches for good.

Give me shelter from doing what I have to and not doing what I should.

Give me shelter from this endless list I can't seem to stop.

Give me shelter from even trying to rhyme this last line and instead just say what's on my mind, that I believe at least right now the true shelter is unconditional love, which if I ever find it I know will shelter me from all of the above.

IN THE HEAT OF THE NIGHT

I wake up, hear a car stop out front, the gate squeaks and then a loud thump as something hits the door. It's *The New York Times.* I love that sound in the middle of the night. It makes me feel secure, even happy. Not just because I know it will be there when I get up in the morning, but because the guy who delivers it cares enough to get out of his car and send it flying all the way to my front door, unlike whoever delivers the *L.A. Times,* which I feel blessed every time it makes it beyond the gutter.

But my heart feels heavy because I know I have to cancel my *New York Times* subscription. Not just because I'm broke again and even that small an expense is a bill I just don't have the money to pay, but because I spend all day reading the newspapers and the magazines people send me in the mail and never get any work done. Like the print junkie I am, I don't just scan a few lines to see what's doing in the world today, I read every word. I even read the business news these days, because I want to know, I long to know, just how my brokeness fits into the scheme of things, and why the money men are backing whoever it might be today. I know what you're thinking, who cares about his newspaper jones, he's lucky to be able to rent a home to have it delivered to.

Yeah, and so are you. Lucky that I'm not like I used to be or I'd pull down those red polka dot pants and pull off that Minnie Mouse shirt and lick you all over till you laughed so hard you had to pee. Or see that dark lady over there with the extensions in her hair and the short skirt and black bare legs in the cowboy boots that make her look like her feet are bare in there too, oh oh oh, what a way to go. Only she's not here with me in the heat of the night and it doesn't feel right to call some *L.A. Weekly* personal for fast phone sex when their message makes it clear they're looking for the same things you are dear—someone to hold them and tell them everything's all right and buy them new clothes and impress them with his tan and car and job and give them a wedding band and adopt their kids by previous marriages and and and maybe I could just slip my hand up that too short dress and confess all the fantasies I've had for the past year every time I think of your soft white skin dear or *your* soft brown in that Betsy Johnson beach gown or—

You want my tuna? Shit, I want *your* tuna! In the heat of the night I want to fish in your stream, I want to stick it in and see if it gets wet, I want to trek your trails and hoist your sails and deliver your mails. I want to wash my face in the places where you get wet. I want to hang ten in your surf, I want to get down like a Smurf and mash my face against your astroturf until it turns blue too. Hey, I'm talkin' to you—every black white brown red pink olive yellow tan beige gray freckled mottled open throttled living cell of every one of you.

I mean, okay, I got a bald spot and some of your friends think I'm a jerk and I sometimes wear torn jeans not because I want to be in fashion but because the only other pair I have aren't clean. I mean in the heat of the night it doesn't matter anyway because I'm usually naked and alone despite the tone of my past poems that make it seem I must have creamed a couple of times a day, not even getting into what goes down on what, in the middle of the night. But I can't get that full figure and the way the moonlight hits it in the curves out of my head, so even though I'm alone in bed that body's somehow right beside me too. Is that what sickos do? Or is that when I add the white-skinned waitress in that little bit of blue who told me I looked better without my glasses. Only I can't see anymore without them. I can't see sometimes even with them. You think I'm looking over your shoulder at some blonde or black-skinned beauty when I'm just trying to rest my eyes from pretending they can see you, without tilting my head back like some aloof snob because these are bifocals and up close it almost hurts to look into your eyes through the main part of the lens.

Aloof! That's what he called me after she called me intimidating! Me aloof? Intimidating? I'm just this guy alone at home in the heat of the night feeling all the fight go out of him as he floats on the rim of a planet that *The New York Times* will bring him up to date on in the morning, until I get the nerve to just say no so that tonight there won't be any soft squeaky gate or soft thud of tomorrow's news but just all the yous who make me dream of new virginities for me to lose in the heat of your night when all the fight has left you too and all you want to do is help me find them.

I Don't Know What to Do

with these feelings
I have for you—
It's funny—I can fake it
with women I'm less
impressed with—write a poem
& send it with flowers—
do all the stuff the charmers do
—but I don't know how to
act on my feelings for you
because it's all so new!
for me—to see someone
so whole & self-contained,
so sweet & yet not needy
(no "help me help me" signals
behind the eyes), so
comfortable with herself
so dignified, sitting across
from me—slow me down God—
I've never seen anyone as
beautiful as her to me—
this vision I've carried
with me for years of the woman
I could finally stop running
away from—though my head
is running away right now
with all the fears I always
hid from women before—

I know, I know, I'm not a kid
anymore—I've seen enough
to know that beauty is more
than a model's knowledge of
how to make her hair & face
glow with fresh ghosts of a
future innocence only children
know—I can do it too sometimes
but tonight I'm all self-conscious
teenage nerves—trying to impress
or regress or—maybe this is progress
God—I am breaking a pattern here—
I can see that at least—
this is where it should have
started—way back when—
instead of instant sex &
craziness—control & trying
to impress with how cool I am—
this way now—being nervous,
excited, crazy in
the teenage first date ways
I skipped over in my drive
to be the prodigy of sensuality—
I mean here I am God,
my hair standing on end from
the static in the air, the
cold & wind & new shampoo
I thought would make my
hair look like I took as
good care of it as hers does—
(that isn't true about the shampoo
but it felt that way
& we all know feelings aren't
fact, but sometimes they're
reality)—only now it's
sticking out (my hair)
in stray gray flares—
like those cartoon characters
who get their fingers stuck
in electric sockets—& then
there's what I chose to wear—

I got so busy I didn't have
time to do the laundry &
the only clean shirt I had
was an Xmas gift from
friends who obviously think
I'm a lot larger—or that
the shirt would shrink—
that's why the collar
even when it's buttoned
closed is hanging halfway
down my neck & sticking way
out—a match for
my traumatized hair—
but at least my slacks &
coat are cool dress-up
kind of gear to wear only maybe
not when she's sitting there in
the jeans & casual stuff
I usually wear—I'm
overdressed—like a hustling
producer trying to impress his
date who doesn't see the way
people stare, wondering what
she's doing with him instead
of the poet who's comfortable
with himself, the way I've
been for a while now God—
until tonight—oh I could
go on forever—my shoes
aren't right & neither is this
restaurant—it's too expensive
& pretentious & full of Beverly
Hills matrons in furs—the
food isn't bad but I can't
taste it anyway—I'm too busy
talking to eat, trying to
repeat a pattern that I know—
that's old & comfortable
even if it doesn't work
anymore—but you obviously
have something else in store

for me man, 'cause I
no longer can make this
pattern work, it's breaking apart
as I sit here feeling my heart
come alive again, & then
noticing the sudden silence, &
becoming afraid she's bored
with me already, even
though you know how
long I've looked for someone
to be quiet with for a change—
could she feel that way too, God?
Does it matter?
Is this about what I'm
breaking through & getting to
on this path you've led
me to? As silly as I feel I'm
being, in this joint, these
clothes, this hair &
nervous chatter—I still feel
grateful for it too man—
because it's innocent and
human—how amazing
that after all those
years of terminal hipness
& street sophistication—
of decadence & despair &
the artificially induced highs
of my g-g-g-generation—
I get a shot at a true reincarnation
—while I'm still in this life—
what a delight God—I don't even
mind if I stay up all night
worrying about what a sight
I must have been, what
kind of impression
I made or failed to make—
it's all worth it God to
know what I'm feeling & to
feel it & to let it be what
it is—a chance to live again

like the curious, excitable,
innocent, loving child I've
always been—but haven't
known or been in touch with
since I can't remember when—
only this time, I get to remember,
because I'm present God, I'm here
& going through it all, eyes open
& the lights on this time—even
if what those lights reveal
is a guy with his hair on end
dressed like he's trying to
close a deal—who knows?
maybe this time I will.

FORBIDDEN FRUIT

all the forbidden fruit I ever
dreamt of—or was taught to
resist and fear—ripens and
blossoms under the palms of my
hands as they uncover and explore
you—and in the most secret
corners of my heart as it discovers
and adores you—the forbidden fruit
of forgiveness—the forbidden fruit
of finally feeling the happiness
you were afraid you didn't deserve—
the forbidden fruit of my life's labor
—the just payment I have avoided
since my father taught me how—
the forbidden fruit of the secret
language of our survivors' souls as
they unfold each other's secret
ballots—the ones where we voted
for our first secret desires to come
true—there's so much more
I want to say to you—but for
the first time in my life I'm at
a loss for words—because
(I understand at last)
I don't need them
to be heard by you.

BAD BOYS AND WOMEN WHO WANT IT ALL

I wasn't bad,
I was just misunderstood.

I wasn't trying to burn down my grammar school.
I was just experimenting out of boredom,
to see how much oxygen it took to keep the
matches going before I slammed my desk shut
on the flames—and one time I waited too long.

But hey, that's how you learn, right?

I was just bored—weren't you?
Isn't that why you wanted it all,
while I got suspended, expelled,
kicked out, arrested, tried, court-
martialed, exiled, 86ed, asked to leave,
fired, let go, walked out on, divorced,
broke, hurt, kicked in the ass, the
heart, the brain, again and again,
knowing all along it was only because
I was misunderstood—but I understood
you, and you understood me, I was
the bad boy and you were the woman
who wanted it all, wanted the flowers
and the poems, the soft caress and
the sweet sweet acceptance of your
getting it all wrong every time you

tried to dress the part or break my
heart because I was too bad when all
you wanted was just bad enough to
make you feel the love was tough
enough to last and still be passionate.
But bad boys don't last, that's
what makes them bad—you can't
depend on them for anything but
not being there when it gets too
square and you want square too
because you are the woman who
wants it all—the lawyer and
the biker bum, the guy who never
leaves and the guy who only knows
how to run. And you think you might
see that in me because I'm slowing
down, I'm learning how to clown
around with the bad boy image
before it gets sad 'cause a guy
ain't a boy no more. I mean bad boys
are one thing but bad old men—
that's something else again,
even when you're the woman
who wants it all.

Ever Notice How

We resist just about everything the other one suggests we do in order to change while we're still in a relationship, but the minute they walk, or more accurately, the minute the breaking-up is accepted and all the rehashing and analyzing and generally hopeless talk is ended, we turn around and start making some changes in our lives that we think are gonna show them and it's weeks or months before we notice that what we've done is exactly what they wanted us to do in the first place and in fact it has made us feel better about ourselves and when we're so much better we think we're over it we can even laugh at the fact that while we've changed for the better thanks to these too-late-to-save-the-relationship alterations in our style and ways—*they*'re still doing the same old stuff that drove us nuts for days but we never admitted, so caught up in being the one who was left and only caring about not being kept by the god of abandonment women seem to articulate best but affects us all nonetheless.

ENTIRELY WILLING

To do what?
Surrender to the dictator
in the little girl smile
of your eyes?
Submit my heart's
elation to the crowd
control of yours?
Ignore the dimpled lies?
Pretend I didn't hear
the dismissive way
you characterize my
human qualities—
as if I was—
or wasn't—all those other
guys you seem to expect
someone—you—or me—
to keep paying for?
I don't play that anymore.
The only kind of
smile I'm entirely willing
to surrender to is the
kind that's kind—&
if you mistake that for
weak or needy, you
must be blind—or you
just haven't been
looking at mine.
Entirely willing?
Try me sometime.

SEXUAL HARASSMENT

I hate it when idiots on the street yell stupid sexual comments at women walking by—it's obviously degrading and disrespectful and if I know the woman it makes me want to kill the son of a bitch. But when you tell me I can't even look, or if I do I can't show any signs of wanting to do anything about it, like live inside that extra skin you call your workout outfit—hey, that isn't sexual harassment.

Sensual harassment maybe, if there is such a thing, 'cause what I'm in the grip of is the cosmic sensuality that drives me to want to explore every nuance of the furniture of your body I'd like to call home. Uh-oh—there I go—that really is kind of sexual harassment isn't it because you haven't given me permission to look at you this way let alone say these things even though I'm the one who says no when we finally get home & you ask me to tie you up & dominate you, in ways I just don't want to anymore.

BREAKING UP IS WHAT

Breaking up is what it sounds like—
is what I know too much about—
and so do you which shoulda been some
kind of clue except that everybody do—
'cause it seems to be part of
the human condition now that the
lifelong commitment tradition is just
an idea we have when we meet but
are glad ain't enforced when we
change our minds by the time we find out
who we really are—not the star of
our childhood dream, but another human
being with all the baggage we got—
a lot these days—like a friend said
on the phone yesterday "everybody's
got shit, we just don't want to be with
someone who's self-righteous about theirs"
and I knew what she meant but it didn't
relieve any pain—to do that I'll
have to fall in love with me again—
then maybe I'll be able to really
do what breaking up implies, I mean
"break *up*," like in higher on the
evolutionary scale is where I want
to be when I finally get ahead to
being me without you defining who
that might be.

I Believe in You

I always do.
Until you do too.
And then,

I got to write it down anyway it comes out today or I'll never write anything because I'm stuck again and I was doing so fine thanks to a new schedule and contact with God and praying and what happened I got all up in my head again with the fantasy of "love" for this woman who is so sweet and womanly and childlike I feel like calling her up right now and going and doing what? I miss *her* too these days, having rediscovered how much I love *her* and what a wimp I was not to tell the world and leave "her" instead of trying to hang out and make something out of a terrible situation that only got worse and oh my my I just can't try so hard any more because it's past my time anyway for doing the prime time stuff, I can get gruff and bluff my way into the part of youngest new old guy around especially if this sweet little thing can make me feel the way she did last night that made me want to bite her off in little pieces and savor them forever does that sound as horrible as I think it does but you know the feeling don't you and it isn't always bad I mean it's such a relief to feel that good again I guess I get too grateful to the women and men who bring that out in me whether it be through support of my work or making out or just a pat on the back I'm way too overgrateful for the crumbs I guess I get, and maybe not grateful enough for the true support that's out there too at any rate I'm happy to be me today, just wish I was in better shape but hey that'll come too, I've been here and there

224

before and I'm not stopping now, no sir, I'm on my way back world, just watch me take this nap, I mean finish this project and snap back—or—maybe not? GOD DOES NOT PUNISH YOU FOR YOUR SO-CALLED SINS, YOU DO! Don't you get that yet? Lighten up man, enjoy yourself, go make a phone call and don't feel all guilty about it, you need to refresh your brain anyway, it's ready to go back to sleep again. Only, don't call *her,* call her, your new-found friend again and again, and hey, whatever you do, be sure and thank God and His grace as it works through you and don't take nothing back alone, and you know you'll always feel at home because that's the real love affair that sustains us in this life, yeah, God is the ultimate wife, if that isn't too blasphemous, maybe what I mean is God is what'll make life with or without a mate as great as you always knew it could be. Oh God thank you for what you are doing for me.

Attitude, Gratitude, and Beatitude

The news all seems bad—
just like it all seemed good only a year or so ago—
the money isn't where we thought it was—
neither are we—
How does it work?
Does anybody know?
Where did the music go?
Did you see Blank Blank's video?
I did this thing I do—I saw this woman and
felt the need to give her all my power—then
I couldn't think of anything but her & getting
her to be my mate because I needed her because
she had the power.

"So what," they say, "that's nothing new."
They think I did the same with you.

I know, it's true that
recessions come & go, like wars, conspiracies,
& music you can really listen to.
What's permanent is—what?
That's what we all would like to know.
It isn't attitude—thank God that changes
as we grow. It isn't gratitude—sometimes
it comes too slow or not at all—& what
the hell is "beatitude" anyway?—another
fancy word for feeling good at nobody's

expense? I call that "love"—the only
guarantee of happiness, & not for me
coming from you, but coming from me
for whatever, if I can let the fear of
loving go—you know—like how you feel
when you just love that song or pet or
painting or book or person or job or joke
or all that stuff you loved so long ago—
or not so long ago. Do it again—let
the fear of loving go—no matter what you
know—because you know this too—that
it is the only way to go to go.

THE CLOUDS

all day today
but especially around 8—
on the way over here
from the beach—
I was thinking about
how when I was a kid
all they hid was sexual to me—
the same promise,
the same secret happiness and
satisfaction I knew would be
mine if I could climb them,
get inside them, like the
women towering over me
with "isn't he cute" &
"my what a big boy" &
"I bet the girls are jealous
of your rosy cheeks" & then
they'd give me a shot of booze
in my tea or a sip of
their beer or a kiss on the
cheek or lips, once even
sticking their tongue in my
tiny boyish cloud-like mouth—
but now I'm at a stop sign
thinking about this poem
I'd like to read tonight
but haven't written yet—

wondering if I'll have time
to get it all down about
how even Nero and de Kooning
were inspired by clouds like
these, Yeats & Robert DiNiro—
running around the Village
as a kid, his father a painter
too & mother a Beatnik matron—
when suddenly I slam on
the brakes just as I'm
pulling out as the third
car runs the stop sign
crossing mine & I hit
the horn & scream
you motherfucker & have
visions of tearing out
his fucking heart
until I see it's an Asian
woman as I finally pull out
& on my way again
remember this poem
& the clouds that
continue to make me
smile at the kid I was
who wanted to climb
them & was so dis-
appointed when in planes
he finally did to see
nothing more nor less than
higher denser fog, except
on top when it was yes
celestial & exhilarating
but not as good as sex
when it did reveal the
secrets I had longed to
know & now I'm
all bogged down in
imagery that brings up
inspirations of my youth
so why is my heart
heavy in the face of

this—I live with a
woman who loves me,
as I do her, I'm paying
off debts a decade old
at last, a book has
finally been accepted,
a record's coming out,
what is my heart afraid
to love, because I
know that's always my
excuse for this deep
apprehension—sure there's
problems in my life as in
the world, though mine
are minor next to
fleeing Rwandans & unlucky
Haitians or Bosnians or
tourists—no—it's always
fear of loving brings me
this kind of pain—
so what could it
be again? it feels so
new—because it
is, I realize as the
clouds absorb me in
their promise & ful-
fillment once again—
it's this—the world
& my life in it that
I fear to lose—a new
fear yes indeed—I'm
so in love with all of
it again & for the first
time understand the
way it all goes on w/out
me when I'm gone—
maybe it's burying another
sibling only weeks ago—a
brother this time—
maybe it's Mother's Day
& mine almost 30 years

gone, my kids' mother
long since passed away
as well—maybe it's
turning 52 when 25
seemed beyond every
prediction I knew—
maybe it's just these
fucking clouds & what
they do to me—bring
all of me home to a
self I finally know—
the knowing, isn't that
the source of all our
longing to express it?
Happy Mother's Day Birth
Michael—let's take a
walk in those clouds someday &
embrace the way that sounds
so final—because
it may well be—

6-5-94

reading—K. asleep—
  browsing in old books—
  in love w/ them again—
  the ways they saved my lives—
still do—my meditation—
    always—O'Keefe a Zen priest—
me the hustler-saint turned
hipster-angel out of proud sinner
of forbidden fantasies—
  & now they're all allowed—
too easy—
        not for me—
I'm done w/ obsessive obsession—
I want to draw & paint &
  play the piano without
    proving anything
      besides
       the natural
        genius
of my kind—
      I act—I wait—I wonder
why it turns out as it does—I think of
those who've gone like Joe last week
or Ed last year or Tim I knew so long
ago—all poets, artists of the word &
  in Joe's case the brush & pencil too—

& you—Lee—Joan—Joan—brother
Jim—I heard the taps—from the
inside of my head—I went to bed
    & saw them there—where I still
live—

Till We Meet Again

for J.B., E.C., T.D., T.B., & J.B.

When we first met
I was still shattered,
recovering from a
marriage where I
felt like the battered one.
I didn't think I'd
ever trust a woman
again. Then I met
you, and I knew behind
that Boston blast
& high tone aspirations
hid a street kid like me,
or how I liked to
think I used to be.

With my kids and
loyal friends and
friendly powers,
you helped put me
back together again.
Your straight talk,
your warrior way
of walking into
lions' dens and
coming out again

with everything intact
& more, a way of
evening the score you
started out so
far behind with.
You bore the scars
from those first hurts
with a survivor's pride,
even though they were all
inside and nobody knew
where they had come from,
except a trusted few,
and the ones who
inflicted them on you.

If you had wanted to
share them, you'd have
needed a week-long mini-series
to give them their due:
beautiful, black-haired,
dark-eyed, sexually abused
& beaten child,
molested & mistreated
by your own big brother
with a poor uneducated
impoverished abandoned-by-
her-drunken-sailor-husband
Brazilian mother,
who hardly spoke English
and never in defense of you
even though you shared
her bed in that too small home,
until you finally fled
to the life they call "the life"
only you did it your way
a self-employed lady of the day,
posing as a freelance coed
in school plaids and knee socks
until the judge put a stop
to that deceit and you flew
even farther away

to an Oxford where
women like you had
never been before,
you left the Boston
business johns for
the British dons
of college greens
where you conned them
into letting you sit in
on classes you could
ill afford or had the
academic background for.

But street smarts count
for something
and what you learned
you knew for good.
And back in the states again
you stood up for kids like you had been,
counseling and protecting them
only to find the doors
to the American dream still locked.
So you concocted some degrees
from Harvard and Oxford
and went where myths like that
are most accepted,
here, in Lalapalooza land
and in no time at all
your name was on the screen
as one of the few women
who make the business part
of show business art come true.

And then you wanted it all,
and felt the call to finally
have a child of your own
to love the way you never knew,
and you found the right stand-up
kind of regular guy to be
the father you never had
to the baby you finally did,

only to find out what really hid inside,
not just the scars, or who knows
maybe it was them, something
from those fucked-up family
genes made you susceptible
to a kind of cancer there was
no defeating or retreating from,
so we all, your friends and guy
and newborn baby boy, watched you
slowly die, with the same kind of dignity
you drew on when you wanted to hide
the past you thought would be
misused or misunderstood.

Yet you were at peace with it at last,
I saw it in your eyes
before you slipped away
maybe because you knew
the circle of deceit and
ignorance, denial and abuse
had finally been broken
and by you, who always,
even in your darkest hour
had a word of encouragement
as straight and tough as you were,
like when you told me before you left for good:
"Stop worrying Michael,
your true friends love you for who you are,
not what you know or where you've been."
Until we meet again.

Or you, my soulmate once
in a transition I still
don't know how to explain.
When we first met I was just
coming out of my own late 20s depression.
You were still in yours,
a veteran like me, only Navy,
where we once thought we knew
the faggots went,
bent on spending their lives at sea

in floating cities of men,
young ones, like you had been.
We shared the Irish-American thing too,
and both were motherless then,
although yours had committed suicide,
a blow you seemed to still be
dealing with when you walked into
the bookstore I helped get started.
It was Washington DC in 1972.
You were in love with poetry
and maybe me, and my wife, and kids,
the family you wished you had.
And we took you in to our mad
long-haired dope-dealing semi-commie
city-hippie last-of-the-Beats
but speed-freak-anal-retentive-neat
commune, where we'd sit around
for days & nights discussing our latest poems,
or the latest challenges to their
political correctness. It was a real home
for all of us, with love and joy
and understanding, but bitter arguments too
about the place of gays and feminism
in our leftist revolutionary communalist brew,
until you shocked us, or at least me,
when one day, seemingly out of the blue,
you revealed your secret love of men,
and then went on to ask me for my support
at a reading you were about to do that night,
at the University of Maryland.
You were excited and afraid,
a high school dropout reading
to an audience of academics and students,
introduced by a well-known straight poet
whose respect you longed to have
but nonetheless chose to "come out" before.
And you did, and I was there,
and where I once saw some kind of
predator enemy I saw you, and then me too,
as the students assumed later we were lovers,
and in a way we were, I loved you,

you loved me, and later, when my wife
insisted I give up my macho poses,
you helped me discover new ones,
like the nice tough guys we really were.
When you moved out and went on with
your new life, we stayed in touch,
and much of what we shared was poetry,
until something changed, but what?
You betrayed a mutual friend,
but then made up for that,
until you and he were close again,
but what happened to us?
I never knew what it was.
You didn't show up for a reunion
of the poetry scene I introduced you to,
you never wrote, you never called,
we grew so far apart I almost forgot
how close we'd been until our friend
called to tell me your heart had stopped.
A stroke—not AIDS or cancer,
not suicide or depression
or the drugs you once had taken for all that.
A fucking stroke at 46, and only then
did I realize what I missed, and even more
when our friend sent me your last manuscript.
You were another great
but overlooked young poet of your time,
your work so simple yet profound,
like I had always meant for mine to be.
Only you did it your way, not mine,
and it was so fine it hurt me to realize
I never told you that.
And now you're gone.
And when I shared this with another friend,
and wondered out loud
what had gone wrong between us,
he reminded me how only once
you had been honored for your work,
and I was hurt that you didn't thank me,
for helping you find your voice, I thought,
for giving you your first reading,

or publishing your first book,
for who knows what all
I thought I had done for you.
Not as much, it seems now,
as you had done for me.
I thought it was you all these years
who had been avoiding me,
and I guess you had been.
Having been hurt by my egotistic need.
And then you were found in your rented room,
alone on the floor,
no phone, no fax machine,
no stereo or car or home or kids.
Nothing except some letters and books
and poems to show for all your work
with the poor and old and homeless
and AIDS-bereaved. And from the
old days a collage of photographs
of your family and friends and you.
They said I was in it too.
And then all by itself,
a picture of my kids
when they were small
and we were all together,
until we all meet again.

Tim was our other mutual friend.
When we read our poetry of
sexual confrontation, he seemed
like just a kid—he told us
we were his heroes.
And now he's gone too, the man who
always reminded me of what I
and my poetry had meant to him,
especially when the bridges
were still burning all around me
and I didn't know how to get out
of my self-inflicted despair.
He was always there.
I published him too his first time out,
and supported him in his conservative

yet secretly flamboyant spirituality.
He mastered many approaches to the
problem of the poem, as well as the
problem of multiple romances.
And he'd share all that with me.
Oh Tim, you helped free me from my demons
just by being there. You understood
my ambitions were just a way to share
my awe and wonder at a world I was
still stunned to be alive in.
I was the one who was supposed to pass.
You were the one I exchanged glances with
when we both found ourselves amidst
the New York literary elite,
glances as if to say, hey, we made it,
now where do we go from here.
I headed West, you North to New Haven.
Me to see how bright my light might be
from where the stars we loved or
made fun of congealed, and you to
see if you could transform your history
into something even more deeply useful
than poetry, and we knew how useful that could be.
You spent years at Yale Divinity,
the last few months of that with the help of a cane.
Pursuing a degree to help you go on to be
a chaplain in an AIDS ward at a hospital in Jersey City
that made Brooklyn, where you first lived alone,
seem pretty. And then you died too,
from that new defenselessness.
Before leaving you wrote
the definitive poem on what
that felt like and appeared on *Good Morning*
or *Today* to read some lines from it.
You looked so secure and strong and
sure of who you were and what you were doing.
Who knew when we first met and you were
then the youngest of our crew
that I would still be here and missing you,
until we meet again.

And what about Ted whose poem
"People who died" started all this,
only his was more or less just a list.
Ted I'm talking to you, as you did
too in your poem to Kerouac,
whom you interviewed just before he died.
An interview we argued about, or I did,
when we first met at that
poet's house in Iowa City in '68
where you had come to teach
and wonder what I was doing there
and not in New York where
you'd already heard of me you said.
I'd heard of you too, and thought
you were a jive self-promoter.
I was so serious in my revolutionary
and self-taught book lover's discoveries
I put down your catering to
the rich patrons of the New York literati,
to help you publish your own work
as well as that of so many others.
But you were so good-natured and honest
in the face of my proto-p.c. zeal,
I couldn't help but give it up
to be friends and acknowledge
without words the lives we shared,
so far from our Irish-Catholic
veteran G.I. Bill of Rights roots.
Later when we were both back in New York,
and I came to visit and talk poetry,
and in the process you found out I was
without the rent again, living alone
with my son in a much nicer place
across town, you got up out of bed,
an unusual occurrence by then, still
talking your speed-driven poetry rap
and I followed you outside and down
the Lower East Side street where
everyone seemed so small next to you
though you weren't so tall you
just walked like you were until

we came up to this bank and you walked
in and kept speed-rapping to me and
whoever was within ear range including
the tellers who all seemed to know
you as everyone on the Lower East Side
did, until you withdrew two hundred
bucks you had just gotten for reading
your poetry somewhere and gave
it to me saying "here" and
me saying, "no, I can't take it you're
as poor as me" and you saying "No,
you need it, I have it,"
and me saying I'll pay you back man
as soon as I can and you saying,
"Michael you don't owe me a thing,
your poetry has given me much more
than two hundred dollars' worth of satisfaction."
And then that big speed-eating grin
full of love and acceptance of me.
And him, I mean you, still smiling
like that years later when I decided
to try out the movie fantasy;
you were one of the few New York
poets who encouraged me, saying it
would have been in your scheme too
if you had been as thin as me, telling
me how to move and what to do and
acting as if I was already there,
not knowing I would end up in despair
out here until I got a call saying
you had passed away finally from all
that speed, not an O.D. just your
body couldn't take it anymore,
in your 40s too, a young man to some
still, and I remember when we both
first moved back to New York in '75
and you said you had come back to die.
So it took you a few more years.
And I decided I didn't want to go
that way, and gave up what my life
was doing to me to come clean, so

I owe you for that one too, Ted.
You were a true friend,
until we meet again.

And Joe. I fell in love with the voice
in your poem "I Remember," in that first
little chapbook with your baby picture
on the cover. And then took the Metroliner
from DC to NYC to hear you read it. I
was in my newfound sexual liberation
period and played it out on you, though
you knew I was faking. The sex was
no good, barely sex at all, and the
intimacy wasn't much better. We were
the same age, same height, same weight,
but so different I couldn't get through.
I wanted to. Just on the strength
of those words you had written,
through which I'd been smitten
and didn't know what to do about it.
We saw each other often when
I moved to New York. Especially
between women I lived with. We
saw each other with them as well,
more socially, and with your friends
and lovers too. But it was the times
we spent alone together that
seemed to matter more to me than you.
Though you were always kind and accepting
of me and my awkward attempts at
some kind of relationship. I wanted
more than close friendship and we
hardly even had that. In
someone else's mind we could have
been lovers. But we just shared the
same space sometimes. I visited
you often, first in your place
on Sixth Avenue over the store right
next to what later became The Limelight.
More frequently at your loft on Greene
Street. I've got a painting you gave me

of your view from the window,
long since gone, new buildings erected
and old ones torn down. Like us. You
always turned our encounters into some
kind of playtime, a game or activity,
probably to keep me from trying to
make it anything more. Sometimes we'd
draw, you me and me you, or parts of
our bodies. One time when we met for
dinner, you handed me a note that suggested
we not talk but instead write to each other.
You had an extra pen and little notepad for me.
It was strange and original and fun. Like
you. I have the portrait you did of Ted B.
in the room where I'm writing this. He
was young and healthy and handsome then.
You caught him perfectly, I feel like he's
looking at me right now, even though
you only drew half his face with one eye.
It's intense. As we sometimes were. There'd
be hours we'd spend with each other and
no words would come. You'd show me your
jewelry collection, gold rings from the Middle
Ages or Renaissance pins. Or the year you
were preparing for a show of your miniature
collages, every time we went out you'd be
constantly picking up debris from the sidewalk
and gutter to take home and arrange not
just by color but shade, so that your loft
became cluttered with subtle variations
of the color spectrum, as though you were
living inside an elaborate rainbow. Once
the show was over you went back to the
simplicity you were a master of. You
kept very little, had more space than stuff.
You were an example to me of living life
with a minimum of possessions.
When I left to go act in movies
I wondered to you why so many
old friends seemed upset with my new turn
of events, I said how we all loved the movies

so much I thought everyone would welcome
my insider insights and you patiently explained
that sometimes in my enthusiasm for my
latest obsession I was like a little puppy
jumping up on to someone's leg, nipping
and yapping and demanding attention,
"cute but annoying" and I understood.
You explained me to myself in a way
that no one else could. Even my work,
and yours, pointing out when I put down
Warhol's gossipy book that any kind
of confession brought solace to someone.
You helped me understand a lot.
Especially in everything you wrote.
I couldn't be you, or even be like
you, or even really part of your scene, no
matter how hard I tried. But I can see
your shy smile right now in my head,
and remember how gently you always
led me back to myself. Thank you for that.
I missed you all those years I was away,
and yet barely wrote or called, but
when I finally did you hid your dying from
me and never complained, just sent
me more books and support and your
love and went on to pretend we'd meet again
soon. Until then.

Addendum

for S.J. & J.H.

I'm back in New Jersey and thinking of you.
Talked to your husband, my buddy, and
one of your sons. He's a good man, you'd
be proud of how well you did. I know
you had trouble with some of your kids
but they all seem okay now. Grown men
and woman with kids of their own.

Your old man is a "senior" now
and still going strong, the last
of that crew who's still standing.
And like me, he did all the dirt they avoided.
It just goes to show. But Sissie, it's
you I miss most. You were always so
kind and bighearted. You loved my
first wife, God rest her soul, and our
kids, but accepted all my crazy changes.
When you first moved to the city from
back home and I'd visit you all in Bed Sty,
you'd have ribs and barbecued chicken
and a six-pack of beer, like my mother
once did. You knew what I liked and
made sure that I had it, and never
stopped laughing at my impulsive
exploits. Your smile could light up
the coldest city night or heart or corner
or life. When you got your house in
New Jersey and I'd come to visit, you'd
laugh at how for years you hadn't known
your old man's pipe wasn't filled with
tobacco. You were a country girl,
an innocent, who could stop
a mugger in his tracks and did
with the glare and the thump of one
tough mama. I'm sorry you're
not here to enjoy your grandkids
and see that even the heaviest night
of your family's soul has grown light.
Jeez I miss you Sissie, more than you
ever could know, though knowing you
you probably did and do. I'm sorry I
wasn't a better friend, and can't wait
till we meet again.

Jim, you just left us after a long
slow decline. The last time we talked
you were anxious to know who else
had passed. As if thinking ahead
of who you might know when you

got wherever it is we go. I was told
in your last weeks you spoke to Gerald
Burns a lot, who dropped dead so
abruptly not so long ago. I guess he
was preparing the way. And then,
I learned that the day before you died
you sat up in bed and
uncharacteristically for you
said "I have seen happiness."
And then said it again. "I have
seen happiness." You were unique.
I knew you from when you were
young, and you still are to me.
I loved your testimony to the
life of a small publisher and poet
that generously included me in.
I loved your Texas drawl, the
slowness of your words and
responses. You didn't care for
a lot I did, but you never hid
your distaste for the ways others
sometimes treated me or reacted
to my life and work. The
way your work was treated
was worse, but you didn't seem
to care or even notice. You wrote
your poems. And rewrote. Mostly
short, and seemingly simple.
Unlike you. Though that's the way
you talked. And seemed to live.
Not true, but a good façade
to disappear behind. Every time
I find some little piece of found
art or poetry and put it aside to
send to you, I have to remind
myself, there's no one there
anymore to send it to, except
in thought, which I do, almost
every day. There's a lot of names
crossed out in my address book.
Your X is new. I miss you man,

but look forward to when we'll
meet again.

There's so many more, a book's
worth in my family alone, and
other poets too, like Elio and
Sharat and Jimmy Schuyler and
you. And so many friends,
Cliff Heard who I had thought
of often but never tried to
reach and when I finally did,
he took me by surprise by
knowing who it was and talking
as though we'd never stopped
a conversation we started in 1960.
Only it was almost 2000, and
he was fading from a cancer
he never mentioned, just said
how he'd been talking to his
girlfriend about me, how he
could see me in Clint Eastwood
kind of movies, he thought we
had a lot in common, tall lean
white men with similar sounding
voices and a thing for jazz. It
was a pleasant compliment.
Especially the naive way he
thought I could just make it
happen. By the time he had
to hang up I hadn't said what
I'd called to tell him, how much
he meant to me, how he was like
a big brother who was there
when I needed him most, how
I loved him. But I let him rest
and called back the following
day, to have his girlfriend say
he'd passed away. I said, "Damn,
I didn't get a chance to tell him,"
and she said that he knew. That
after I hung up he said to her,

"That boy really loves me you know,
I was like a big brother to him."
To him, and you and all the other
long gone members of my family
and recently departed friends,
you're in my heart and head and
words until we meet again.

So I Went to Minneapolis

They were having a benefit and asked me to read at it and convinced me it mattered if I did; so I told them I would. I was away at the time—on vacation with my daughter, my son, and my new daughter-in-law. First at a family reunion in New Jersey, where over a hundred showed up, and I got to stand around in a small circle of grayheads like me. We had all grown up on the same street when we were kids together, and we knew the legends in our memories were true, and now here we were together again, and it was extraordinarily tender in a way only we could see, and I was so happy to see it.

My children too, who never knew the family I knew, except on rare visits, found like-minded cousins with styles they could recognize and appreciate as something of their own, and in that, a home they could own like I never did, except here in the words that were always my closest companions. And then on to Ireland where relations they'd never seen created a feeling of home never known, yet always known. It was there I agreed on the phone to read at the benefit in Minneapolis.

So only two weeks after I got back to my little monk's room in Santa Monica, I got on a plane again. When I got off, there was no one to meet me. I called and they seemed sorry but okay with that idea. They knew someone would eventually show up and all I had to do was wait. But they couldn't know who I was waiting with—that old ego doom I had known so intimately for years, as I watched my various careers disappear into fantasies of revenge.

I mean, just before I left for Minneapolis, I got a call about the day job that paid the rent—the commercials I appeared in—

after a lifetime of seeing me, in my mind, striding across the big screen, showing the world how a poet might do whatever the reigning stars were doing. I'd heard stories for years from friends and poetry fans of how they felt I'd sold out, seeing the jobs I chose to do to support my kids as not as worthy for a poet as the ones they did. It didn't matter anymore. My kids were grown and long gone. My son married now, my daughter just moved to Massachusetts and the country I never introduced her to.

So the agent who handled my day job for me said *he* wants you—the best of the ones who direct those things—*he* wants you for his new one and they shoot it this week. But I'll be in Minneapolis I told her, and she said okay I'll tell them you can't do it, unless they pay you—and here she quoted a figure more than ten times what I usually get, and I asked what we'd do if they agreed. She said they wouldn't, but if they did it'd be a new place to negotiate from, and so much, I could get in touch with Minneapolis and tell them I had to stay in L.A. for a job but could donate what it would cost to make up for my not being there.

I told her I had to know right away because I was leaving in two days. She called back to say they had offered to double my usual pay, and when she said no only more than ten times that would do, they said they'd let her know but never called back, which always means no. So, I let Minneapolis know I was coming and the next day they Fed-Exed my ticket, but then my agent called to say, you won't believe this, they've agreed to pay what we asked for, and I said oh shit, I'm committed to this Minneapolis thing.

But she asked me to stay and make this dough I'd maybe never see again unless I did, because it could turn things around— I might finally be financially secure. I said let me call Minneapolis and get back to you, but she said no, they need to know now, they're on the other line, you have to decide. I prayed a fast question to the God I rely on and the answer I got was go to Minneapolis, so I did.

And now here I was after that cramped little space they call a place on a plane these days, and in this new to me terminal, and no one to greet me, where I had only been once decades before, in uniform, in a bar, in the snow of a faraway winter's day. Not this one. It was August outside in a way I hadn't experienced. I was finally paged and went searching for my host and found him with another writer and soon we were on our way to Minneapolis, or actually St. Paul, after first dropping off the other writer in what looked like a condo complex all modern and air-conditioned and comfortable.

When we got to our destination, the generosity there would have normally comforted me, but all I could see was the air that despite the fierce ways it sometimes moved was hotter than any I'd experienced before. And I couldn't stop thinking about all the money I'd turned down to come to this town in heatwave hell.

And I couldn't stop telling anyone who'd listen, wanting them to know what a sacrifice I'd made, mister martyr burning at the Minneapolis stake. If it was only that simple, but it never is when we do what we believe God is suggesting. Like the big TV interview they'd planned, that partly enticed me to come, was canceled for reasons beyond their control, so now they had a madman on their hands and had to find something to do with me.

So we go to see the "Beat" exhibit I wouldn't see before if it was next door, but at least it was air-conditioned, something I never thought I needed before. Reluctantly, I felt grateful for the cool air as we walked through the exhibit I already hated and then hated more as it fed my self-righteous proprietary feelings—about a time I thought I owned—by including John Coltrane as connected to the "Beats," who turned my little Jersey soul onto the truth of my desires and then shot me down when I came around to their parties and hangouts as a little bebop hophead they couldn't get in bed or out of their hair or under control when I'd get drunk on their wine and step through somebody's bass and be hated for acting like Kerouac supposedly did but without his credentials, just working-class Catholic child of immigrant culture too, with hidden writings accumulating back in Jersey against the dictates of my father who wouldn't believe our street had more perverts and secret sins and violence than Greenwich Village of 1950's innocence.

And now here they were, the bastards who hadn't let me in back then, like Ted Joans, with his white wife and half-white kids trying to hit on my black girl in those days while putting me down as an interloper, as if my love wasn't as sincere as his, the phony in a beret reading to tourists in the phony cafes like "Wha?" near where I eventually lived with older black guys who never hid their desire for Miss Ann or made fun of mine for Sapphire. Ah, all the phonies I had to deal with back then and here they are again, in pictures and words in this famous Minneapolis museum on this scorching day and me regretting the dough I left behind that might show these pricks what I'd done to get beyond their scorning of my too jitterbug Jersey kid ways.

But then, seeing the little monitor rerun of Kerouac's famous *Steve Allen* set, the purity of Jack's vision and honesty coming through, the genius of that stance in a land gone frightened of the truth, goddamn I love that man and all he was and stood for. So my heart is open thanks to Kerouac and his reading, as I round a corner and walk right into—how could it be?—I'm thinking, they found one of my old collages, the ones I made to keep me company in the service back then, where I ran away to when that black girl said I wasn't enough, or maybe it was me I was running from, or the rejection from those Beatnik bastards.

It didn't matter anymore because here was one of those crazy collages I used to make on the backs of thrown-out guitars or old Chinese room dividers or doors or whatever was handy to glue and paint some images to, only now as I get closer I see this one wasn't made by me but by somebody else I've never heard of as part of this scene before and the door to my heart opens even wider as I suddenly realize, like in one of those epiphanies Joyce was always writing about, how there must have been thousands of us back then finding a way to be new to ourselves and the truth we all stumbled on—it's just that a handful of us got noticed for whatever reasons of promotion or connections or coincidence or luck or ... Who cares? Not me, as I see they just represent me and the rest of us doing our best in those days to be honest.

And once again I experience the God I relate to, who I'd been testing again and again in my mind with my resentment about listening to Him or Her and coming to this town, turning down a small fortune to do it. But here I am, standing in front of this almost ugly collage from so long ago, letting go of an even older resentment against those who didn't know how deeply they'd hurt me. They were just people, like this unknown collagist, and the one I had been, only more famous for doing what hundreds of us had done to survive a time of lies and confusion, like any time.

And then there was more, as there always is when I walk through the doors that God opens. Because in the next room was a monster of a painting, the surface sometimes a foot thick with oil and whatever held it in place, a sensual star of light and fecund material that brought up fantasy's secret desires, and close by photographs of the naked artist spreading her legs to show us her inspiration. And then in a dark little cubicle, a silent black-and-white film of her watching them take that painting away—and in her small size and her way of moving and looking and dressing, I saw my wife back then and remembered the little dark Beatnik chick she had been and how much I had dug it and her—and another resentment went flying as though released from between the backs of my shoulders, like it had been binding my wings, and things fell into place in my heart and my head like they hadn't for years and I felt the tears come to my eyes.

I was smiling too, happy to love her again, remembering when we were young and proud of our outlaw condition the others made famous but we made our lives. Until hers ended and I got religion in my own way, long after the day we had parted not friends anymore. Okay. I get it God, I had to come here and be overwhelmed with the heat to be talked into seeing this show, taking this seat in this dark little room, so I could know the truth of that time was just as much mine and hers as theirs. And I don't have to be angry at them anymore.

Then, before we left I looked at the rest of the show and felt a kind of beneficence toward it, remembering finally how I had loved it all and been inspired by even the ones who had scorned me in their ways. There were still more days to spend here but now I was ready to go, having learned the lesson God had in store. Only, as I keep finding out, there is always more, until there is no more. The job I'd turned down continued to inspire dissatisfaction, even as I enjoyed the jazz I was taken to hear—Shirley Horne proving something about age I needed to know, and the late-night talks reconnecting me with my host and his mate in ways that brought back another time and the seekers of truth who made it distinct, that 1960s hippie extension of hophead delight in all things mysterious, or obvious, and it was as fulfilling as then, again, catching up with where it might be now, in these younger companions of another outlaw way.

But wouldn't you know it, by the time the benefit happened, I was back again in that place of disappointment and revenge, especially when I realized it wouldn't have mattered if I wasn't there, if I was back making the fortune I'd forgone. And then two poets whose work I dug responded to mine with such precise praise, I felt so gratified I got that this was my life and what I had always done and did to make it mine. So okay, God, I get it, once more.

255

And then my last day, I read at a local bookstore, but before I'm driven there, I see a name I'd never forgotten and ask where it came from, this man I'd assumed dead long ago from the ravages of war and oppression. Oh no, he's alive, in fact, he lives here in Minneapolis. So I call and hear through his accent a man I remember, though he's not sure of me, until he is. I have a picture of him at the party for my daughter's christening, in Iowa City of 1968. We were students and dug each other and our work, though he once told me there was too much "shit" in mine. Literally, the word "shit" too much in my poems, when the world had enough already.

Which he soon proved by returning to his homeland to win an election and fly to the U.N. to broker a peace he felt so proud of only to go home to find an even worse curse on him and his people as Pol Pot's little devils began to cultivate their killing fields with him high on their list. But he tricked them by acting insane, like I had years ago on the streets of Harlem when gangs seemed to threaten my life and I remembered a story about prospectors who pretended to be crazy to keep Indians from killing them and it worked.

As it did for my friend, threatened with so much worse than a gang beating or even torture or death by scalping. First he destroyed, before they could, everything he owned, his entire home, except for one poem of Emily Dickinson's he needed as a reminder of another way of life that transcended the "shit" he was living with—he hid it by burying it, as though giving poetry the funeral Pol Pot meant for all things beautiful.

When he told me all this, my heart missed a beat in awe of the power of a poem. It helped keep him alive when they killed his father and then his wife and daughters. He survived by using his own shit this time, spreading it over his body, so the little boy devils would pass over him in their torturous games. And it worked. He was even able to save his son at a nearby camp by sneaking him raw bits of a kind of Cambodian crawfish he'd catch in the dark of night, as though guided by an unseen light inside his heart, and fingers, and passion to survive to keep his son alive.

Now they're both in the U.S., where my friend flies to cities, or in the twin ones, to speak to our homegrown devil boys in their Cambodian gangs. He's succeeded in turning some of them around—one notorious gang leader in California became a Buddhist monk! And as he tells me all this, after hearing me read with my still "too much shit," I feel blessed and fortunate, beyond the petty little desires of the jobs and money left behind, so I ask him why he thought he survived, and he smiles and looks upward to heaven, and I nod and smile back at him.

But even so, by the time I get back to my little home, I'm fighting to stay grateful and not be depressed by the money I'm still thinking I let pass. For a week I sit on my grief over what I thought I'd lost, until another agent who oversees the voice-over work I do, asks how my trip to Minneapolis was, and I say great but can't help relate how I gave up "a fortune" to go there.

So she asks what job I'd turned down, and when she hears, her eyes open wide in an "oh no" stare as she makes clear how it would have been a "conflict" if I had done it—in fact the job that paid my bills that year could have sued me for their share of everything I earned and the one I'd have stayed to do could have made me give back that fortune I thought I would have missed by not doing it.

So by *not* staying and doing it, I had kept myself from instant poverty and more debt than I'd ever had, even in my poorest poet years. But instead, here I am again, shaking my head in wonder at the gift of prayer—one simple request had sent me on a quest for relief from years of misconceptions and misbeliefs, and saved me from my petty greed and insecurity, by showing me once more how the only door that matters is the one to the heart, and how, coming in or going out, it works best when it's open.

More Than Enough

there's more than more than more than
more than enough so why isn't enough enough and where is it
written that enough will never be enough except
in the amazing arrogance of societies and
institutions and governing bodies of immune deficiency
allowances of tabloid mentalities that breeed breeeed
breeeeed breeeeeed breeeeeeeeeeeeeeeeeeeed infinity when
all we are asking for is food.

all we are asking for is enough space to live a life of
enough space to enough space to live a life of gratitude

when all we are asking for is no more hope no more dope no
more ways of being anything less than the stewards of all
that god has created including each other which means
caretakers which means taking care of which means caring for
each other and every other living thing and everything *is*
living from that star that is supposed to have died so many
thousands of years ago and yet still shines in your eyes to
that grain of sand in the shoe of the man sleeping on the rock
of all our past discouragement—

I'm talking about the reason we are here today
to look at each other and say what can I do for you
to help you get through whatever lack is causing you pain or
sadness or fear or anger or feelings of victimization—

there is only one nation, and it is the nation of
love, we weren't wrong in the '60s we were just too
self-righteous about it thinking whatever made us shout
also gave us the clout to have it all our way so I ask
today for the humility of the saints and the bodhisattvas,
the courage of the martyrs and the *Kama Sutra* the love of
every god who ever gave solace to any lonely soul like
mine and yours, I am reassured by that love no matter how
many tanks and guns and chemical weapons our collective
greed has ignited in the hearts of even lonelier souls who
have no recourse but belligerence and death to satisfy the
myth of their invulnerability—

we are all vulnerable, today's success stories, tomorrow's
homeless, let us all be warriors for love as if we were
sent from above to heal these wounds of neglect, because,
hey, guess what—we were.

AND THEN THERE WAS HER

I remember women lining up
to dance with me, not so long ago.
Now I simply sway and move in place
trying not to seem self-conscious
of the 23-year-old who looks so sexy
in her white silk pajamas, or whatever
the fashion term is for the outfit
I can see her figure through
and the skin I knew one night
I shouldn't have discovered
for as much as I was satisfied
with barely touching as
her almost one night lover
and she too claimed to be.
But she is married, and
he's here, and I almost feel
sick being aware of that.
God forgive me.

I am insane with desire
for this 23-year-old wife,
I know I can't be with (again).
My obsession with thoughts
of "her" again—though new—
and "wrong" though no contact
on my part, just mental, and heart.
The mystery of desire and distraction.
I am so tired, and still, as so often
throughout my life, I cannot sleep.

∞

Woken by a noise, frightened for my new car—the first I ever bought myself, or could—my "baby." Now awake thinking of her as I was last night and the night before after telling her we can't even talk on the phone because it isn't "right." And yet all I want to do is talk to her all night, every night, on the phone, in bars and cars and bed. My head knows from experience and life I did "the right thing." My heart and other parts resist that "truth" with all their might, telling me to recover her number and call and if her husband answers hang up. And so I wait for it all to pass: the pain, the irregular heart, the anxiety and anger, the not giving a shit about anything except thoughts of her—and us—and ... And every time the phone rings my heart leaps like some teenage girl in love. How quaint. How queer. How fucking tiresome my uncontrollable yearnings for a woman I can't be with. How I don't care tonight I want her here right now and wish she'd call again despite my saying not to.

∞

Saw her tonight. After many sleepless nights the obsession broke and the battles with my demons—and God. But now it's the sadness, the loss, of what? Excitement, connection, satisfaction, intimacy, the whole deal. So, tonight, felt empty to see her, like something missing in my life. It was difficult, and yet, just seeing her satisfied something. I'm such a kid still in my heart, waiting for the romance of my life to start at last. She was frail, even fragile, as her husband helped her walk and move around. Her hand grabbing his, or patting his head, tugging on his ear as I tried not to watch. Her dark eyes darker from her pain and progress back to life in ways she couldn't know were so close to those I always chose. And I know again how much alike we are and cannot be. I see her pale white hands holding her cigarette and drink and think maybe someday she'll see me in her when I'm gone or just a memory that flashes in some younger man's face or gesture as I see myself in hers. I adore her now for real. No not-knowing. No not-wanting. I acknowledge my debt to her face and form which holds some of the secrets I was always searching for or trying to share from me. Now she's the one in ways I find startling and unsettling and I don't want to make a living or be responsible or mature. I want to wallow in these feelings of discovery, of success in the quest for the secret promise I once thought all women share. But no, it's only there, tonight, in her, so unaware of how much it means to me.

∞

She's leaving her husband, for which I feel guilty, afraid, and I have to admit excited. We haven't been together in any sexual way and tried to cut off all contact several times. But then we'd see each other socially and she'd call and we'd talk for hours—all that teenage stuff. I know it will most probably lead to pain, and sound insane to others. Over thirty years difference, all the obvious problems, kids (she wants them, I already raised mine), etc. But. Ah, the "but." I guess I'm still too weak in this area. I haven't given in to getting together in any physical way, have even avoided going to see her when she's wanted me to. But, I have stayed on the phone for hours, and yesterday I walked in Venice with her and her friends, the only ones who know, she says, and then we spent some time together alone, just talk and silence, and holding occasionally, like a quiet, unmoving kind of dance. A lot of deep breaths and sighs. I know it sounds high schoolish. Am I really so susceptible to—what? Romantic addiction. I'm afraid of losing my friends' respect, and my children's. I keep praying and asking for help. And then still answer the phone and we talk and connect.

∞

She's been here almost every night and each one has been happier than the one before. I feel like I've never been happier in my life. I am so in love. She is so like me in so many ways. Some I've outgrown or outlasted, that once left me angry or insecure and then I acted out or withdrew. Maybe our love for each other will keep us both satisfied until it becomes something even greater. Things only get better the more time we're together. This is the most unconditional and nonjudgmental love I've ever had for anyone besides my kids, which is maybe why I feel they may be threatened by it.

∞

Saw the baby on ultrasound—a boy—moving and jumping around. As active and demanding already as us. We're good together I think.

262

She's strong enough to just say what she thinks no matter what, as I used to do, or wanted to, and our arguments are brief and well matched and that's that. I love her deeply, and marvel at that sometimes—and already deeply love our child as well. Life is so unpredictable, thank God! We went to SF for me to pick up an award for my poetry from P.E.N. or more specifically Bob Callahan who introduced me saying all I could have asked for. And when I started to read my Jackie Robinson poem about my father, she said the baby started jumping around inside her, excited by my voice, or *for* me, as I was. Distinguishing among all the other readers and recipients in a crowd of a hundred and fifty or more. My boy! As I've felt with my other son, and daughter, so many times. And now him. Frolicking inside his mom in ways we can see from outside! So fucking brilliant is this creative process, everything else seems—well ... I feel so at home with it all, despite the bumps and brief encounters with conflict. There is no doubt we are here and meant to be.

∞

Still beautiful, our love, our life together. I marvel at how all this has evolved in ways I cannot control nor want to. I have never been so happy with a woman than I am with her. Our relationship just deepens with each day. Her capacity for growth and change always amazes me. That she can see so clearly and quickly her own need to develop and find new ways to deal with her own "defects" puts my lifelong attempts to shame. And the baby is so beautiful and full of passion he makes my heart ache with love and the deep desire to be there for him every moment of his life. Sometimes I wish she were my age and we had met in 1956 and never parted. To which she counters she wouldn't have liked me as I was back then, or any time much before the man I have become. Sounds true. I'm just so grateful that she found me and our son found both of us.

LALLY'S ALLEY REVISITED

And so I moved back, a few blocks away and forty years later. My grandfather's house is still there. But the old Esso station next door is now a Blimpie's. The A&P where he got his booze has expanded to incorporate what once was Mister Bombosidi's house. The tiny makeshift rundown "Italian Mediterranean" stucco bungalow, with his beautiful garden and statue of Our Lady is now the produce section. The little railroad widows' cottages at the bottom of the street, closest to the tracks, are now all parking lot.

The bowling alley building is still there, but where the diner was is now Vinnie's Nails in neon in the window. The alleys where we bowled are apartments, and the lanes downstairs where only men were allowed, once full of cigar smoke and the broken legs of pinsetting boys who didn't get out of the way fast enough, are garages for the apartments. The roundhouse where we watched them turn engines around, and the hobo camp are now all parking lot too, for the giant Pathmark where the old lumberyard once stood.

My young wife tells me to "get over it," when for the millionth time I reminisce about what's wrong with all the changes, as if they could be reversed, or should be. My last name is still on the mailbox at the house where I grew up, the ex-wife of a cousin who grew up next door lives there with a few of their grown kids. One's waiting to get on the force, like my grandfather (his great), and his father, and all the other Lallys who once reigned there.

Another cousin tells me at a recent reunion that there was a time when not only our street was known as "Lally's Alley," but also the one a block over, where three other uncles had their families before I was born. That must have been where her father crawled to the candy store from, after the attempted suicide that finally succeeded. He'd called my father after he'd done it, but my father thought it was another cry of "wolf" from the boy who was always lying, and so didn't respond and never got over it.

The candy store now sells liquor too, and isn't owned by a German named Joe as it was when my uncle died there, or later by the Jewish man we called "shellshock Sam" because he had St. Vitus Dance disease, which we always ascribed to battle fatigue whether the man was a veteran or not. It's owned now by Indians, or maybe they're Pakistanis, being as difficult for me to tell apart as Northern Irish Protestants would be for them from Southern Catholics.

I keep expecting to run into someone I know. But every time I think I recognize a person, I realize they'd be old and gray-haired now. That sort of generic senior look I'm reluctantly growing into. Like the time I went into the old delicatessen—one of the few places almost still the same as when I left here forty years ago—to get their famous Sloppy Joe (more like a Dagwood sandwich than the slop known elsewhere by that name) and ask about one of the most standup guys I knew back when we were kids. He was a few years older and lived on the other side of town, but ran with some of the guys from my neighborhood because he had a cousin there.

His father used to make the sandwiches at this deli when I was a kid working in my father's two-by-six-foot storefront around the corner, answering the phone and repairing old toasters and irons, or stapling new screening into an old wooden frame. I looked around the deli for someone who might remember my friend or his father but everyone looked too young. Then I spotted this old balding gray-haired guy leaning over a meat slicer and figured he'd know.

You've already guessed I'm sure, it was my old friend. It took him a minute to recognize, or maybe even remember me. But when he did he was the same regular guy, as nice as he could be. He's still a legend in my mind, though he talked about himself like he was the old bump on a log and I was the free spirit who had to leave home. He even used those words.

Said it was natural for him to still be at the same job and for me to have roamed the world and changed careers, or at least jobs, as often as I moved, or more. But he's the one who married the hottest girl we knew when we were all hitting puberty. Every guy in town wanted her. And she dated a few, especially the guys with big ambitions or families that we knew as "rich."

But he was just this decent hardworking guy. And she chose him. They had tons of kids, six I think, and then she split. And he raised them. A thing I always thought I was such a pioneer of, having raised my two oldest mostly by myself back when he was doing the same with three times as many and in his usual way not taking any credit or seeking any.

Now he's a part owner of the deli and has remarried with a few more stepkids to take care of. And me remarried too, with a two-year-old of my own, and a beautiful wife who is the love of my life and probably doesn't really know it, no matter how many times or how many ways I find to tell her or show it.

The store around the corner from the deli where I spent every afternoon and all day Saturdays for most of my high school years is long gone. The old 19th-century wooden building that had me daydreaming back then about how it was when it was like a cowboy place—with wooden sidewalks and all, like when my father was a boy, though it's New Jersey after all and not the Wild West—was torn down. The whole corner has disappeared, transformed into some kind of mini-rest-station, or parklet, or whatever. Some bricks to make the sidewalk look more quaint, some benches and stone flower pots.

Across from where it was, the old cigar store is still there, where Big John, or John the Cigar, stood behind the tiny counter, a Cuban as big as his arm hanging from his lips and sold me "The Bible" as my father and his pony-playing friends called *The Daily Armstrong* racing form. Big John liked my ambition and my smarts. He had a tender heart, for an Italian who looked like he could wipe the floor with anyone who came through the door and sometimes did.

He'd let me borrow any new paperback I wanted to, as long as I didn't crack the spine or dirty the pages. I'd read them in my father's store when business was slow and then return them. The cigar store has expanded since then, and seems to sell more lottery tickets than anything else. No paperback book racks anymore. I asked the owner, another Indian or Pakistani, how long they'd been there. He said fifteen years ago his father bought the place from an old, but still very tall, Italian man named John.

Next door to him is a black hairdresser. Then a Chinese

266

takeout, a tiny Caribbean restaurant, and like that. A regular United Nations of small businesses. The whole town's that way. Where the businesses once were dominated by old WASP money and *nouveau riche* Jewish dough, the place is dramatically more African and Caribbean, with a mix of Asian and Near Eastern thrown into the stew.

It makes me grin to see the chickens have come home to roost, and found a coop more friendly to the kind of kid I was when I ran so hard and fast to get away from here. But now I'm back, and as I hear the sound of an old piano and tap dancing coming from the open windows of the dance school above the cigar store, and see the range of hues on the skin of passersby, I almost want to cry that my father couldn't be here to see how it all turned out, for now. The way I thought it would.

At night I still listen to the sound of the trains passing by, but no longer the rattling freight trains of my childhood, instead much smoother-sounding commuter trains that go all the way to Penn Station in New York, and have for two years now. The reason local real estate has taken off, with people who can no longer afford Brooklyn or Long Island, let alone Manhattan, moving in. Of course the realtors make sure they stay away from my old neighborhood. Too risky, in their terms, both safety- and investment-wise. Though still much safer than our next-door neighbor, Newark, where, even there, some parts are almost hip these days.

Coming out of the parking lot behind the old A&P one night, passing the red-brick condominium apartments already aging, where when I was a kid a Kaiser-Frazer car dealership had been, I finally get it. It's okay, this change. To some kid growing up here now, this will be what makes the place tick, what makes his background special and unique, what makes his street unlike these other streets that to a stranger might all look alike. And even if it doesn't, it doesn't matter.

What matters is watching my kid run through the legs of grownups at a christening for some distant kin. The mostly Irish mugs of his cousins and uncles and aunts and various in-laws, with a few darker-hued thrown in. Even an African from the mother country in the extended family now. With an accent so British and proper it makes me grin to hear the contrast with the Jersey din of dropped consonants and elided participles and all the rest that made me identify with the Bowery Boys when I was a kid.

267

A kid growing up on my street now most likely wouldn't even know who Bing Crosby is, or was, the man who in his Irish-Americanness represented our best intentions and redemption. That kid more likely sees Lauryn Hill the way we did Bing Crosby, and Hill doesn't live a continent away like Bing once did, but only up "the hill" where newly rich white ethnic groups aspired to not so long ago.

It's a new world, and yet the same old one. Where family matters most, and ethnicity is still the butt of jokes, and dysfunction is as familiar as the beer and booze that flows. But the things that have changed have all changed for the better, as I know my grandfather felt, having grown up in a dirt-floor, thatched-roof cottage filled with kids and pigs and a meal made out of potatoes. He never looked back. I still do, and am grateful for it all.

It Takes One to Know One

One what?—

Nigger, kike, wop, honky, paddy, redneck, frog,
cocksucker, bastard, bitch, motherfucker, dog—
punk, nerd, dweeb, sissy, jerkoff, creep,
queen, faggot, bulldyke, Republican sheep,
right-wing, leftist, Trotskyite, capitalist pig,
facelifted faketitted phony-in-a-wig,
impotent, premature ejaculator,
stand-up comic, poet, actor,
waiter, chauffeur, screenwriter, masturbator,
sibling, in-law, spouse, kid, victim, manipulator,
codependent, alcoholic, addict, abuser,
liar, cheater, thief, quitter, loser,
photographer, reporter, lawyer, dealer,
doctor, chef, model, hair stylist, healer,
quack, booshie, commie, jock, gambler, gangster,
fuck-up, greed head, homie, rambler, prankster,
hippie, yuppie, beatnik, artist, freak,
monster, asskisser, cartoonist, geek,
hoser, dickhead, wanker, slant-eyed dwarf,
fatso, pasty-face, nothin-but-soft,
sexist, racist, agist, whore,
Buddhist, born-again, sober bore,
white, brown, yellow, red, black and blue,
he, she, them, us, it, me, you,
rocks, mountains, clouds, trees,

269

rivers, valleys, inlets, seas,
birds, horses, whales, kittens, bees ...
Hey!—
This could go on forever,
when all we really gotta say is:
Everything and us—

Us
       and
              everything—

from the smallest quark
to the biggest galaxy—
it's all the same,
and it only takes one
to know one.

One what?

Printed July 2001 in Santa Barbara &
Ann Arbor for the Black Sparrow Press by
Mackintosh Typography & Edwards Brothers Inc.
Text set in Plantin by Words Worth.
Design by Barbara Martin.
This first edition is published in paper wrappers;
there are 200 hardcover trade copies;
100 hardcover copies have been numbered & signed
by the author; & 22 copies lettered A–V
have been handbound in boards by
Earle Gray & are signed by the author.

PHOTO: Robert Zuckerman

Born in Orange, New Jersey in 1942, youngest of seven in an Irish-American family of cops, priests, and politicians, MICHAEL LALLY started out playing piano and reading his poetry in coffeehouses and bars in 1959. In 1962 he joined the Air Force, where he spent over four years as an enlisted man, and later used the G.I. Bill to attend the University of Iowa Writers Workshop. During those years he wrote the autobiographical *South Orange Sonnets,* which on publication led to a New York Poetry Center Discovery Award in 1972.

Lally's first book was published in 1970. By 1980 there were twenty, including the 1974 poetry collection, *Rocky Dies Yellow,* and the 1978 collection of prose and poetry, *Catch My Breath.* In 1974 he received a National Endowment for the Arts Poetry Award, the same year he wrote a long autobiographical poem, *My Life,* which on his receiving his second National Endowment for the Arts Poetry Award in 1981, was denounced as pornography on the floor of the United States Congress by politicians out to discredit and dismantle the NEA.

Lally moved from Manhattan to L.A. in 1982 to find work acting in movies and TV, mostly as a bad guy (like a psycho detective on *JAG*), and the occasional good guy (a gentle artist on *NYPD Blue*), while his writing found its way into several movies. In 1997 *Cant Be Wrong,* a collection of poems, won a PEN Oakland Josephine Miles Excellence in Literature Award.

In 1999 Lally moved home to New Jersey and Black Sparrow Press published a collection of poetry and prose, *It's Not Nostalgia,* which won an American Book Award and in 2001 Black Sparrow published another collection of poetry and prose, *It Takes One to Know One.*